THE AMERICAN MILITARY

Opposing Viewpoints

THE AMERICAN MILITARY

Opposing Viewpoints

David L. Bender

Greenhaven Press

577 Shoreview Park Road
St. Paul, Minnesota 55112

© Copyright 1983 by Greenhaven Press, Inc.

ISBN 0-89908-317-X Paper Edition
ISBN 0-89908-342-0 Library Edition

"Congress shall make no law...
abridging the freedom of speech,
or of the press."

first amendment to the U.S. Constitution

The basic foundation of our democracy is the first amendment
guarantee of freedom of expression. The *Opposing Viewpoints
Series* is dedicated to the concept of this basic freedom and the
idea that it is more important to practice it than to
enshrine it.

CONTENTS

Chapter 4: Is a Draft Necessary?

Why Consider Opposing Viewpoints?

"It is better to debate a question without settling it than to settle a question without debating it."

Joseph Joubert (1754-1824)

The Importance of Examining Opposing Viewpoints

The purpose of this book, and the Opposing Viewpoints Series as a whole, is to confront you with alternative points of view on complex and sensitive issues.

Probably the best way to inform yourself is to analyze the positions of those who are regarded as experts and well studied on the issues. It is important to consider every variety of opinion in an attempt to determine the truth. Opinions from the mainstream of society should be examined. Also important are opinions that are considered radical, reactionary, minority or stigmatized by some other uncomplimentary label. An important lesson of history is the fact that many unpopular and even despised opinions eventually gained widespread acceptance. The opinions of Socrates, Jesus and Galileo are good examples of this.

You will approach this book with opinions of your own on the issues debated within it. To have a good grasp of your own viewpoint you must understand the arguments of those with whom you disagree. It is said that those who do not completely understand their adversary's point of view do not fully understand their own.

Perhaps the most persuasive case for considering opposing viewpoints has been presented by John Stuart Mill in his work *On Liberty*. Consider the following statements of his when studying controversial issues:

> If all mankind minus one were of one opinion, and only one person were of the contrary opinion, mankind would be no

9

more justified in silencing that one person than he, if he had the power, would be justified in silencing mankind. . . .

We can never be sure that the opinion we are endeavoring to stifle is a false opinion. . . .

All silencing of discussion is an assumption of infallibility. . . .

Ages are no more infallible than individuals; every age having held many opinions which subsequent ages have deemed not only false but absurd; and it is as certain that many opinions now general will be rejected by future ages. . . .

The only way in which a human being can make some approach to knowing the whole of a subject, is by hearing what can be said about it by persons of every variety of opinion, and studying all modes in which it can be looked at by every character of mind. No wise man ever acquired his wisdom in any mode but this.

Pitfalls to Avoid

A pitfall to avoid in considering alternative points of view is that of regarding your own point of view as being merely common sense and the most rational stance, and the point of view of others as being only opinion and naturally wrong. It may be that the opinion of others is correct and that yours is in error.

Another pitfall to avoid is that of closing your mind to the opinions of those whose views differ from yours. The best way to approach a dialogue is to make your primary purpose that of understanding the mind and arguments of the other person and not that of enlightening him or her with your solutions. One learns more by listening than by speaking.

It is my hope that after reading this book you will have a deeper understanding of the issues debated and will appreciate the complexity of even seemingly simple issues when good and honest people disagree. This awareness is particularly important in a democratic society such as ours, where people enter into public debate to determine the common good. People with whom you disagree should not be regarded as enemies, but rather as friends who suggest a different path to a common goal.

Analyzing Sources of Information

The Opposing Viewpoints Series uses diverse sources; magazines, journals, books, newspapers, statements and position papers from a wide range of individuals and organizations. These sources help in the development of a mindset that is open to the consideration of a variety of opinions.

The format of the Opposing Viewpoints Series should help you answer the following questions.

1. Are you aware that three of the most popular weekly news magazines, *Time, Newsweek,* and *U.S. News and World Report,* are not totally objective accounts of the news?
2. Do you know there is no such thing as a completely objective author, book, newspaper or magazine?
3. Do you think that because a magazine or newspaper article is unsigned it is always a statement of facts rather than opinions?
4. How can you determine the point of view of newspapers and magazines?
5. When you read do you question an author's frame of reference (political persuasion, training, and life experience)?

Many people finish their formal education unable to cope with these basic questions. They have little chance to understand the social forces and issues surrounding them. Some fall easy victims to demagogues preaching solutions to problems by scapegoating minorities with conspiratorial and paranoid explanations of complex social issues.

I do not want to imply that anything is wrong with authors and publications that have a political slant or bias. All authors have a frame of reference. Readers should understand this. You should also understand that almost all writers have a point of view. An important skill in reading is to be able to locate and identify a point of view. This series gives you practice in both.

Developing Basic Reading and Thinking Skills

A number of basic skills for critical thinking are practiced in the discussion activities that appear throughout the books in the series. Some of the skills are described below.

Evaluating Sources of Information: The ability to choose from among alternative sources the most reliable and accurate source in relation to a given subject.

Distinguishing Between Primary and Secondary Sources: The ability to understand the important distinction between sources which are primary (original or eyewitness accounts) and those which are secondary (historically removed from, and based on, primary sources).

Separating Fact from Opinion: The ability to make the basic distinction between factual statements (those which can be demonstrated or verified empirically) and statements of opinion (those which are beliefs or attitudes that cannot be proved).

Distinguishing Between Bias and Reason: The ability to differentiate between statements of prejudice (unfavorable, preconceived judgments based on feelings instead of reason) and

11

statements of reason (conclusions that can be clearly and logically explained or justified).

Identifying Stereotypes: The ability to identify oversimplified, exaggerated descriptions (favorable or unfavorable) about people and insulting statements about racial, religious or national groups, based upon misinformation or lack of information.

Recognizing Ethnocentrism: The ability to recognize attitudes or opinions that express the view that one's own race, culture, or group is inherently superior, or those attitudes that judge another race, culture, or group in terms of one's own.

It is important to consider opposing viewpoints. It is equally important to be able to critically analyze those viewpoints. The activities in this book will give you practice in mastering these thinking skills. Although the activities are helpful to the solitary reader, they are most useful when the reader can benefit from the interaction of group discussion.

Using this book, and others in the series, will help you develop basic reading and thinking skills. These skills should improve your ability to better understand what you read. You should be better able to separate fact from opinion, substance from rhetoric. You should become a better consumer of information in our media-centered culture.

A Values Orientation

Throughout the Opposing Viewpoints Series you are presented conflicting values. A good example is *American Foreign Policy.* The first chapter debates whether foreign policy should be based on the same kind of moral principles that individuals use in guiding their personal actions, or instead be based primarily on doing what best advances national interests, regardless of moral implications.

The series does not advocate a particular set of values. Quite the contrary! The very nature of the series leaves it to you, the reader, to formulate the values orientation that you find most suitable. My purpose, as editor of the series, is to see that this is made possible by offering a wide range of viewpoints which are fairly presented.

David L. Bender
Opposing Viewpoints Series Editor

Introduction

"In the councils of government, we must guard against the acquisition of unwarranted influence, whether sought or unsought, by the military-industrial complex. The potential for the disastrous rise of misplaced power exists and will persist."

Dwight D. Eisenhower, Farewell Address to the American People, January 17, 1961

A nation's military exists, in principle, to insure that nation's safety from foreign and domestic threats. In America, as in virtually all modern democracies, military forces are subject to strict civilian control. The consequences to any nation of its military establishment moving beyond civilian control are obvious and ominous.

When President Dwight D. Eisenhower delivered his now nearly legendary farewell address, he was alerting Americans to what he perceived as the possible threat to democracy from the growing political power of the American military and its allies in Congress. He emphasized the need for all citizens to remain alert and knowledgeable in order to "compel the proper meshing of the huge industrial and military machinery of defense with our peaceful methods and goals, so that security and liberty may prosper together."

Events since that address in 1961 appear to have justified Mr. Eisenhower's concern. In a recent article in the *Los Angeles Times*, political analyst Rone Tempest wrote that the military-industrial complex is creating "political constituencies that make 'captives' of congressmen, state officials, labor unions and even presidents, who often support questionable military spending out of fear for their political lives." He continued by noting that "under such pressure, the built-in 'checks and balances' of American government repeatedly break down."

Current statistics offer evidence of the power and pervasive nature of the United States military establishment. Defense spending provides the major source of income for one out of ten

Americans. Defense industries account for 10 percent of all manufacturing in the United States and employ over 25 percent of America's engineers and scientists. Finally, the Pentagon pays for more goods and services than any other single purchaser in the nation.

These statistics, however, do not necessarily lean in the direction of military "overkill." There are many people, both in and out of government, who allege that, relative to the strength of its enemies, the American military falls short in strength and influence. In his Annual Report to Congress for the 1983 fiscal year, Secretary of Defense Caspar W. Weinberger offered an imposing picture of the military might of the Soviet Union. He stated that "the Soviet military industry has grown steadily and consistently over the past 20 to 25 years. Its physical growth and the commitment of large quantities of financial and human resources is its most dynamic aspect." America, on the other hand, is experiencing "serious deficiencies in [its] military forces."

This anthology of opposing viewpoints attempts to deal with four significant issues related to the possible dangers of and/or need for a strong American military. The questions debated are: Are U.S. Military Forces Adequate? Is the U.S. a Militaristic Society? Is Military Spending Harmful? and Is a Draft Necessary? The importance of these questions cannot be overstated. Whether by choice or necessity, America's military establishment has become a fundamental part of a complex and massive international military machine. And regretfully, the political, economic and ideological chasms separating the governments which underwrite this military machine only serve to intensify the complexity.

Are U.S. Military Forces Adequate?

THE
AMERICAN
MILITARY

"When I took office in January 1981, I was appalled by what I found: American planes that could not fly and American ships that could not sail."

Soviet Superiority Threatens U.S. Security

Ronald Reagan

On March 23, 1983, President Ronald Reagan appeared on national television to speak to the American people about peace and national security. He spoke about the need to rebuild America's defenses and the necessity of increasing defense spending. The President claimed that while the Soviets accumulated enormous military might during the past 20 years, American defense forces deteriorated. The following viewpoint, which is excerpted from the President's speech, claims that if America wants to remain free and preserve peace it must increase defense spending.

As you read, consider the following questions:

1. What does President Reagan mean when he says the defense debate is "not about spending arithmetic"?
2. What evidence does the President present to support his claim that the Soviets have pulled ahead of the U.S. in military might?
3. How do the Soviets threaten U.S. vital interests, according to the President?
4. How does the President appraise Soviet intentions to use their military power?

Ronald Reagan, speech delivered from the White House, Washington, DC, on March 23, 1983.

I want to explain to you what this defense debate is all about, and why I am convinced that the budget now before the Congress is necessary, responsible and deserving of your support. And I want to offer hope for the future.

But first let me say what the defense debate is not about. It is not about spending arithmetic. I know that in the last few weeks you've been bombarded with numbers and percentages. Some say we need only a 5 percent increase in defense spending. The so-called alternate budget backed by liberals in the House of Representatives would lower the figure to 2 to 3 percent, cutting our defense spending by $163 billion over the next five years. The trouble with all these numbers is that they tell us little about the kind of defense program America needs or the benefits in security and freedom that our defense effort buys for us.

What seems to have been lost in all this debate is the simple truth of how a defense budget is arrived at. It isn't done by deciding to spend a certain number of dollars. Those loud voices that are occasionally heard charging that the Government is trying to solve a security problem by throwing money at it are nothing more than noise based on ignorance.

We start by considering what must be done to maintain peace and review all the possible threats against our security. Then a strategy for strengthening peace and defending against those threats must be agreed upon. And finally our defense establishment must be evaluated to see what is necessary to protect against any or all of the potential threats. The cost of achieving these ends is totaled up and the result is the budget for national defense.

There is no logical way you can say let's spend X billion dollars less. You can only say, which part of our defense measures do we believe we can do without and still have security against all contingencies? Anyone in the Congress who advocates a percentage or specific dollar cut in defense spending should be made to say what part of our defenses he would eliminate, and he should be candid enough to acknowledge that his cuts mean cutting our commitments to allies or inviting greater risk or both.

Our Policy Is to Deter Aggression

The defense policy of the United States is based on a simple premise: The United States does not start fights. We will never be an aggressor. We maintain our strength in order to deter and defend against aggression – to preserve freedom and peace.

Since the dawn of the atomic age, we have sought to reduce the risk of war by maintaining a strong deterrent and by seeking

17

genuine arms control. Deterrence means simply this: Making sure any adversary who thinks about attacking the United States or our allies or our vital interests concludes that the risks to him outweigh any potential gains. Once he understands that, he won't attack. We maintain the peace through our strength; weakness only invites aggression.

This strategy of deterrence has not changed. It still works. But what it takes to maintain deterrence has changed. It took one kind of military force to deter an attack when we had far more nuclear weapons than any other power; it takes another kind now that the Soviets, for example, have enough accurate and powerful nuclear weapons to destroy virtually all of our missiles on the ground. Now this is not to say the Soviet Union is planning to make war on us. Nor do I believe a war is inevitable – quite the contrary. But what must be recognized is that our security is based on being prepared to meet all threats.

The Present Situation

For two decades, the Soviet Union has been engaged in building up the most powerful military forces in all man's history. During this period, the United States limited its own military spending to the point that our investment in defense actually declined in real terms while Soviet investment was nearly double our own during the decade of the 1970s.

President Ronald Reagan before the American Legion on February 22, 1983.

There was a time when we depended on coastal forts and artillery batteries because, with the weaponry of that day, any attack would have had to come by sea. This is a different world and our defenses must be based on recognition and awareness of the weaponry possessed by other nations in the nuclear age.

We can't afford to believe we will never be threatened. There have been two world wars in my lifetime. We didn't start them and, indeed, did everything we could to avoid being drawn into them. But we were ill-prepared for both – had we been better prepared, peace might have been preserved.

The Soviet Buildup

For 20 years, the Soviet Union has been accumulating enormous military might. They didn't stop when their forces exceeded all requirements of a legitimate defensive capability. And they haven't stopped now.

During the past decade and a half, the Soviets have built up a massive arsenal of new strategic nuclear weapons – weapons that

can strike directly at the United States.

As an example, the United States introduced its last new intercontinental ballistic missile, the Minuteman III, in 1969, and we are now dismantling our even older Titan missiles. But what has the Soviet Union done in these intervening years? Well, since 1969, the Soviet Union has built five new classes of ICBM's, and upgraded these eight times. As a result, their missiles are much more powerful and accurate than they were several years ago and they continue to develop more, while ours are increasingly obsolete.

The same thing has happened in other areas. Over the same period, the Soviet Union built four new classes of submarine-launched ballistic missiles and over 60 new missile submarines. We built two new types of submarine missiles and actually withdrew 10 submarines from strategic missions. The Soviet Union built over 200 new Backfire bombers, and their brand new Blackjack bomber is now under development. We haven't built a new long-range bomber since our B-52's were deployed about a quarter of a century ago, and we've already retired several hundred of those because of old age. Indeed, despite what many people think, our strategic forces only cost about 15 percent of the defense budget.

Another example of what's happened: In 1978, the Soviets had 600 intermediate-range nuclear missiles based on land and were beginning to add the SS-20 – a new, highly accurate mobile missile, with three warheads. We had none. Since then the Soviets have strengthened their lead. By the end of 1979, when Soviet leader Brezhnev declared "a balance now exists," the Soviets had over 800 warheads. We still had none. A year ago this month, Mr. Brezhnev pledged a moratorium, or freeze, on SS-20 deployment. But by last August, their 800 warheads had become more than 1,200. We still had none. Some freeze. At this time Soviet Defense Minister Ustinov announced "approximate parity of forces continues to exist." But the Soviets are still adding an average of three new warheads a week, and now have 1,300. These warheads can reach their targets in a matter of a few minutes. We still have none. So far, it seems that the Soviet definition of parity is a box score of 1,300 to nothing, in their favor.

So, together with our NATO allies, we decided in 1979 to deploy new weapons, beginning this year, as a deterrent to their SS-20's and as an incentive to the Soviet Union to meet us in serious arms control negotiations. We will begin that deployment late this year. At the same time, however, we are willing to cancel our program if the Soviets will dismantle theirs. This is what we

have called a zero-zero plan. The Soviets are now at the negotiating table – and I think it's fair to say that without our planned deployments, they wouldn't be there.

Now let's consider conventional forces. Since 1974, the United States has produced 3,050 tactical combat aircraft. By contrast, the Soviet Union has produced twice as many. When we look at attack submarines, the United States has produced 27, while the Soviet Union has produced 61. For armored vehicles including tanks, we have produced 11,200. The Soviet Union has produced 54,000, a nearly 5-to-1 ratio in their favor. Finally, with artillery, we have produced 950 artillery and rocket launchers while the Soviets have produced more than 13,000, a staggering 14-to-1 ratio.

There was a time when we were able to offset superior Soviet numbers with higher quality. But today they are building weapons as sophisticated and modern as our own.

The Threat to Our Vital Interests

As the Soviets have increased their military power, they have been emboldened to extend that power. They are spreading their military influence in ways that can directly challenge our vital interests and those of our allies. The following aerial photographs, most of them secret until now, illustrate this point in a crucial area very close to home – Central America and the Caribbean Basin. They are not dramatic photographs but I think they help give you a better understanding of what I'm talking about.

This Soviet intelligence collection facility less than 100 miles from our coast is the largest of its kind in the world. The acres and acres of antenna fields and intelligence monitors are targeted on key U.S. military installations and sensitive activities. The installation, in Lourdes, Cuba, is manned by 1,500 Soviet technicians, and the satellite ground station allows instant communications with Moscow. This 28-square mile facility has grown by more than 60 percent in size and capability during the past decade.

In western Cuba, we see this military airfield and its complement of modern Soviet-built MIG-23 aircraft. The Soviet Union uses this Cuban airfield for its own long-range reconnaissance missions, and earlier this month two modern Soviet antisubmarine warfare aircraft began operating from it. During the past two years, the level of Soviet arms exports to Cuba can only be compared to the levels reached during the Cuban missile crisis 20 years ago.

'THIS WAY YOU CAN SIT DOWN AND TALK'

Don Hesse, *St. Louis Globe-Democrat*. Reprinted with permission.

This third photo, which is the only one in this series that has been previously made public, shows Soviet military hardware that has made its way to Central America. This airfield with its MI-8 helicopters, antiaircraft guns and protected fighter sites is one of a number of military facilities in Nicaragua which has received Soviet equipment funneled through Cuba and reflects the massive military build-up going on in that country.

On the small island of Grenada, at the southern end of the Caribbean chain, the Cubans, with Soviet financing and backing, are in the process of building an airfield with a 10,000-foot runway. Grenada doesn't even have an air force. Who is it intended for? The Caribbean is a very important passageway for our international commerce and military lines of communication. More than half of all American oil imports now pass through the Carib-

21

bean. The rapid build-up of Grenada's military potential is unrelated to any conceivable threat to this island country of under 110,000 people, and totally at odds with the pattern of other eastern Caribbean States, most of which are unarmed. The Soviet-Cuban militarization of Grenada, in short, can only be seen as power projection into the region, and it is in this important economic and strategic area that we are trying to help the governments of El Salvador, Costa Rica, Honduras and others in their struggles for democracy against guerrillas supported through Cuba and Nicaragua.

These pictures only tell a small part of the story. I wish I could show you more without compromising our most sensitive intelligence sources and methods. But the Soviet Union is also supporting Cuban military forces in Angola and Ethiopia. They have bases in Ethiopia and South Yemen near the Persian Gulf oilfields. They have taken over the port we built at Cam Ranh Bay in Vietnam, and now, for the first time in history, the Soviet Navy is a force to be reckoned with in the South Pacific.

The Question of Soviet Intentions

Some people may still ask: Would the Soviets ever use their formidable military power? Well, again, can we afford to believe they won't? There is Afghanistan, and in Poland, the Soviets denied the will of the people and, in so doing, demonstrated to the world how their military power could also be used to intimidate.

The final fact is that the Soviet Union is acquiring what can only be considered an offensive military force. They have continued to build far more intercontinental ballistic missiles than they could possibly need simply to deter an attack. Their conventional forces are trained and equipped not so much to defend against an attack as they are to permit sudden, surprise offensives of their own.

Our NATO allies have assumed a great defense burden, including the military draft in most countries. We are working with them and our other friends around the world to do more. Our defensive strategy means we need military forces that can move very quickly – forces that are trained and ready to respond to any emergency.

The Neglect of American Forces

Every item in our defense program – our ships, our tanks, our planes, our funds for training and spare parts – is intended for one all-important purpose – to keep the peace. Unfortunately, a

decade of neglecting our military forces had called into question our ability to do that.

When I took office in January 1981, I was appalled by what I found: American planes that could not fly and American ships that could not sail for lack of spare parts and trained personnel and insufficient fuel and ammunition for essential training. The inevitable result of all this was poor morale in our armed forces, difficulty in recruiting the brightest young Americans to wear the uniform and difficulty in convincing our most experienced military personnel to stay on.

There was a real question, then, about how well we could meet a crisis. And it was obvious that we had to begin a major modernization program to insure we could deter aggression and preserve the peace in the years ahead.

We had to move immediately to improve the basic readiness and staying power of our conventional forces, so they could meet – and therefore help deter – a crisis. We had to make up for lost years of investment by moving forward with a long-term plan to prepare our forces to counter the military capabilities our adversaries were developing for the future.

I know that all of you want peace and so do I. I know too that many of you seriously believe that a nuclear freeze would further the cause of peace. But a freeze now would make us less, not more, secure and would raise, not reduce, the risks of war. It would be largely unverifiable and would seriously undercut our negotiations on arms reduction. It would reward the Soviets for their massive military buildup while preventing us from modernizing our aging and increasingly vulnerable forces. With their present margin of superiority, why should they agree to arms reductions knowing that we were prohibited from catching up?

Believe me, it wasn't pleasant for someone who had come to Washington determined to reduce Government spending, but we had to move forward with the task of repairing our defenses or we would lose our ability to deter conflict now and in the future. We had to demonstrate to any adversary that aggression could not succeed and that the only real solution was substantial, equitable and effectively verifiable arms reduction – the kind we're working for right now in Geneva.

Thanks to your strong support, and bipartisan support from the Congress, we began to turn things around. Already we are seeing some very encouraging results. Quality recruitment and retention are up, dramatically – more high school graduates are choosing military careers and more experienced career personnel

23

are choosing to stay. Our men and women in uniform at last are getting the tools and training they need to do their jobs.

Ask around today, especially among our young people, and I think you'll find a whole new attitude toward serving their country. This reflects more than just better pay, equipment and leadership. You the American people have sent a signal to these young people that it is once again an honor to wear the uniform. That's not something you measure in a budget, but it is a very real part of our nation's strength.

It will take us longer to build the kind of equipment we need to keep peace in the future, but we've made a good start.

We have not built a new long-range bomber for 21 years. Now we're building the B-1. We had not launched one new strategic submarine for 17 years. Now, we're building one Trident submarine a year. Our land-based missiles are increasingly threatened by the many huge, new Soviet ICBM's. We are determining how to solve that problem. At the same time, we are working in the Start and I.N.F. negotiations, with the goal of achieving deep reductions in the strategic and intermediate nuclear arsenals of both sides.

We have also begun the long-needed modernization of our conventional forces. The Army is getting its first new tank in 20 years. The Air Force is modernizing. We are rebuilding our Navy, which shrank from about 1,000 in the late 1960's to 453 ships during the 1970s. Our nation needs a superior Navy to support our military forces and vital interests overseas. We are now on the road to achieving a 600-ship Navy and increasing the amphibious capabilities of our marines, who are now serving the cause of peace in Lebanon. And we are building a real capability to assist our friends in the vitally important Indian Ocean and Persian Gulf region.

This adds up to a major effort, and it is not cheap. It comes at a time when there are many other pressures on our budget and when the American people have already had to make major sacrifices during the recession. But we must not be misled by those who would make defense once again the scapegoat of the Federal budget.

The Cost of Defense

The fact is that in the past few decades we have seen a dramatic shift in how we spend the taxpayer's dollar. Back in 1955, payments to individuals took up only about 20 percent of the Federal budget. For nearly three decades, these payments steadily increased and this year will account for 49 percent of the budget.

By contrast, in 1955, defense took up more than half of the Federal budget. By 1980, this spending had fallen to a low of 23 percent. Even with the increase I am requesting this year, defense will still amount to only 28 percent of the budget.

The calls for cutting back the defense budget come in nice simple arithmetic. They're the same kind of talk that led the democracies to neglect their defenses in the 1930's and invited the tragedy of World War II. We must not let that grim chapter of history repeat itself through apathy or neglect.

Yes, we pay a great deal for the weapons and equipment we give our military forces. And, yes, there has been some waste in the past. But we are now paying the delayed cost of our neglect in the 1970's. We would only be fooling ourselves, and endangering the future, if we let the bills pile up for the 1980's as well. Sooner or later these bills always come due, and the later they come due, the more they cost in treasure and in safety.

This is why I am speaking to you tonight – to urge you to tell your Senators and Congressmen that you know we must continue to restore our military strength.

If we stop midstream, we will not only jeopardize the progress we have made to date – we will mortgage our ability to deter war and achieve genuine arms reductions. And we will send a signal of decline, of lessened will, to friends and adversaries alike.

"No nation in history has ever been encircled with more firepower than the Soviet Union is today – and we are tightening that circle constantly."

U.S. Superiority Threatens World Peace

Sidney Lens

After President Reagan's March television address, critics reacted. Among them was Sidney Lens, senior editor of *The Progressive* magazine and author of *The Maginot Line Syndrome: America's Hopeless Foreign Policy*. Mr. Lens claimed that total blame should not be placed on the Soviets for the arms race and that America should shoulder much of the responsibility for the dismal situation in which both superpowers are mired. In the following viewpoint the author claims the president failed to make a case for military buildup and misled the American public with his scenario of overwhelming Soviet superiority.

As you read, consider the following questions:

1. Why does the author think the U.S. should have negotiated a nuclear freeze or a cutback in 1968?
2. What evidence does Mr. Lens present to refute President Reagan's claim of Soviet superiority?
3. How does Mr. Lens respond to the President's claim that American military forces are defensive and Soviet forces offensive?

Sidney Lens, "What the President Didn't Tell Us." Copyright 1983 Christian Century Foundation. Reprinted by permission from the May 4, 1983 issue of *The Christian Century*.

The substance of the president's claim was that the Russians are moving ahead of us. In the past decade and a half, he said, the Soviets "have built up a massive arsenal ... that can strike directly at the United States." The fact is that in the past decade and a half, *both* powers have built up a massive arsenal. In 1968 the United States had 4,200 strategic nuclear warheads, the Soviets 1,100; today we have 9,300, they have 7,300 – an increase of 5,100 for us and 6,200 for them.

What those figures prove is not that we need "more," but that we should have negotiated a freeze or a cutback in 1968, before our escalation sparked their escalation. Former Secretary of Defense Robert McNamara – by no means an apologist for the Kremlin – told the *Los Angeles Times* in 1982 that the Soviet buildup of the 1960s and 1970s was a "reaction to the earlier U.S. military buildup and to rumors that the U.S. was preparing to strike first at the Soviet Union. ... If I had been the Soviet secretary of defense I would have been worried as hell at the imbalance of forces."

What President Reagan Didn't Say

As proof that the Russians are plunging ahead of us, Reagan produced a graph showing that the most recent new missile in our arsenal, the Minuteman III, was introduced in 1969, whereas the Soviets have developed and produced five new missiles since then. It sounded frightening, as though we had become militarily impotent.

But while it is true that we haven't built a new type of missile, we introduced the MIRV (multiple independently targetable re-entry vehicle) in 1970, so that land-based missiles which once carried only a single warhead now carry three, and those on submarines, as many as 14. Of greater importance, our weapons now have guidance systems such as the MARV and the MARK 12-A, which make them at least twice as accurate as Soviet weapons. This development is of the utmost importance, for if the accuracy of a weapon is doubled, its "kill" capability increases by eight times.

The difficulty in making nuclear comparisons is that each side has different weapons for different strategies. Reagan made much ado about Soviet superiority in intermediate-range missiles. They had 600 before, he said; they have added hundreds of the new SS-20s – whereas the United States still has no such weapons at all in Europe, "none." "So far," he chided, "the Soviet definition of parity is a box score of 1,300 to nothing in their favor."

The president omitted a few pertinent facts, however. One is

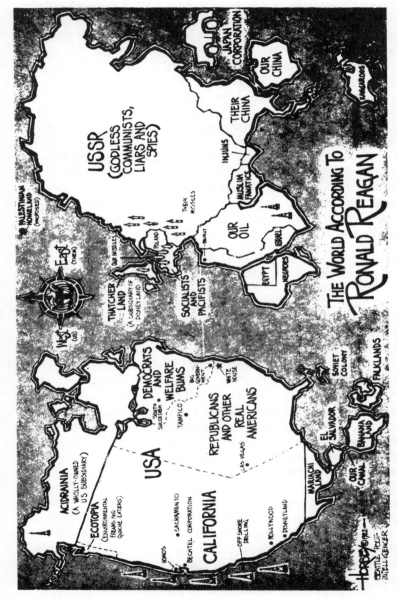

David Horsey, *Seattle Post-Intelligencer*. Reprinted with permission.

that the U.S. has a large number of F-111 airplanes in Britain capable of raining hundreds of nuclear bombs on the Soviet Union. Our allies, Britain and France, also have a few hundred warheads each (mostly on submarines), capable of hitting the Soviet Union. And although most of our 7,000 tactical nuclear warheads in Europe do not have the range to reach Soviet soil, we have a couple of dozen submarines in the Atlantic, Pacific, Mediterranean and Indian oceans which have at least 3,000 warheads targeted on the U.S.S.R. all the time – plus 2,000 more in home ports.

Our 41 nuclear submarines are invulnerable – which means that, unlike the situation with land-based missiles, no way has yet been found to track them down and destroy them. The Soviets also have nuclear submarines, of course, 61 of them, but almost all of their missiles carry single warheads; few are fully MIRVed. Thus the ratio in the United States' favor is nearly five to one – 5,000 submarine-launched warheads for us, a thousand or 1,200 for them. Moreover, most Soviet ships of this class are in port; they have only 400 nuclear weapons at sea at any given time.

U.S. Has Soviet Union Surrounded

To emphasize how menacing the Soviet threat has become, Reagan showed classified pictures of a Soviet intelligence-gathering facility in Cuba, run, he said, by 1,500 Soviet technicians, and another in western Cuba for long-range Soviet reconnaissance. He also showed a 10,000-foot airstrip on the island of Grenada (population 110,000) being built by Cuba with Soviet help. These three facilities are supposed to represent a grave threat to American security.

A little reflection indicates how out of focus such claims are. The Russians may or may not have two bases and one airstrip near American soil. But the U.S. has had bases with nuclear weapons flush up against Soviet territory, in Turkey, for decades. Our troops and ships are ensconced in 400 major and 2,000 minor bases around the world, most of them part of a great circle around the Soviet Union. No nation in history has ever been encircled with more firepower than the Soviet Union is today – and we are tightening that circle constantly.

American Nuclear Threats

Reagan implied that our military machine is benevolent, for defensive purposes only; the Soviets' is malevolent, for offense. "Some people may still ask, 'Would the Soviets ever use their for-

America's Paranoia

Paranoia is no less destructive in international relations than in personal relations. The history of this nation's relationship with the Soviet Union since 1945 provides clear evidence of paranoia in foreign policy. For the past 35 years, our dominant perception of the Soviets has read this way: limitless appetite for aggression; unrestrained use of military power and terrorism; lying and chicanery; cynical repression of human rights.

It is not surprising that this sinister view of the Soviets has led us to adopt a policy that has depended primarily on weapons and minimized the use of political, economic, and diplomatic strategies. As a 1950 National Security memorandum stated so succinctly, the Soviets despise compromise and "understand only force." The consequence of our nefarious view of the Soviets, which mirrors their sinister view of us, has been an arms race that has brought the entire planet to the brink of a nuclear Armageddon.

If we think about U.S. and Soviet relations from another perspective – one which realistically acknowledges Kremlin-generated violence and repression, but doesn't start with the assumption the Kremlin is the earthly headquarters of Satan – we can consider the Soviet predicament. On its western flank, the Polish economic and political revolt has surely weakened Soviet influence over other Eastern European satellites. Western European countries have agreed to provide bases for 108 Pershing II missiles and 464 cruise missiles which will be aimed at Soviet cities and military installations. On its southern flank, the fundamentalist Islamic revolution which has swept through Iran and other Moslem countries threatens to roll into the Soviet Union, igniting the religious passions of the 50 million Islamic people who live within the Soviet borders.

The ill-considered Soviet invasion of Afghanistan apparently was intended to deal with this Islamic agitation. Unexpectedly, it has turned into a Soviet re-enactment of Vietnam. The USSR cannot pull out without turning the country over to a hostile government. If it stays, it will continue an expensive and bloody war in which it cannot win a clear-cut military or political victory. To the East, the Soviet Union faces China and the prospect that tens of millions of Chinese soldiers could some day soon stand on its border armed with U.S. weapons.

After looking at these facts, we can draw some conclusions about the Soviets that are very different from those which inform our paranoid stereotype of them. First, the Soviets are not all-powerful; the Soviet bear cannot rampage at will throughout the world. Second, what some perceive as aggressive actions may, in large measure, be defensive actions designed to protect the Soviet Union from very real military and revolutionary threats located at its borders. Third, there may be elements of our national behavior that bring out the worst in the Soviets which, in turn, provoke us into further destructive actions.

Darel Grothaus, "The Danger In Chirps and Mutters," *Sojourners*, March 1983. Reprinted with permission from *Sojourners*, P.O. Box 29272, Washington, DC 20017.

midable military power?' Well, again, can we afford to believe they won't?" He pointed to Afghanistan and Poland, two instances in which the Soviets come off badly. But he omitted our own interventions in Lebanon, the Dominican Republic, Vietnam, our hundreds of covert CIA actions and – most grave – the 12 known occasions when the United States has considered or threatened limited or total nuclear war.

The first such instance, reported by Senator Henry Jackson more than 30 years after the event, occurred in 1946, when President Harry Truman gave Soviet Ambassador Andrei Gromyko a 48-hour ultimatum for the Russians to get out of two provinces in Iran, or have the Soviet Union itself atom-bombed. In October 1962 we again threatened nuclear war against the Soviet Union because it had placed missiles in Cuba. And in 1973 the superpowers almost came to a nuclear exchange when the Israelis were slow to observe a cease-fire in the Yom Kippur War.

Then there were nine occasions when limited nuclear war was planned or threatened: twice during the Korean War (once by Truman, once by Eisenhower); once in Vietnam, when we offered three nuclear bombs to France to use on China and the Viet Minh; a second time in Vietnam when our marines were surrounded at Khe Sanh; and yet a third time when Nixon sent secret messages through intermediaries that he would use nuclear weapons against North Vietnam unless the Vietnamese came to terms by November 1969. We weighed using the bomb to force the communists to join a tripartite government in Laos, to defend Quemoy and Matsu islands against China, during the Berlin blockade and during the 1957 "Lebanon crisis." Given this history, for Reagan to imply that only the Soviets contemplate using armed force and nuclear weapons – whereas we are quiescent – is more than a gross exaggeration.

The president failed to make a case for his requested $30 billion boost in the 1984 military budget, even from the point of view of a hawk. He didn't mention that we already have enough strategic warheads to destroy all 218 Soviet cities with a population of 100,000 or more at least 40 times over; and that the only purpose additional weapons might serve would be, in Winston Churchill's phrase, to "make the rubble bounce." . . .

Conclusion

Each side is furiously building its arsenal, and shouting that the other is untrustworthy. The U.S., for instance, is projecting 100 new B-1 bombers, 100 MX missiles, 15 Trident submarines, 464 ground-launched and 8,348 air- and sea-launched cruise

missiles, 108 Pershing II missiles, 1,280 neutron bombs and two new aircraft-carrier battle groups – and the U.S.S.R. is no doubt matching us bomb for bomb. Also in the meantime, other nations are gaining the capability of making nuclear weapons – 100 nations are expected to be members of the "nuclear club" by the year 2000 – and the danger of a nuclear war beginning in a "small" conventional way – say, between Iran and Iraq – is growing apace. Germany and Japan can begin producing nuclear weapons within a couple of months after they make the decision to; if the present trade frictions intensify, the possibility that other great powers will join the nuclear club mounts.

Against this background, Reagan's speech is seen not as a plea for strategic arms reduction but for making the U.S. so overpowering that Moscow would have no alternative but to cry uncle. That is the hope – though not the likelihood.

The arms race can be ended only by ending it. That means an immediate freeze without quibbling over the niceties of "verificaton." Better still is Jerome T. Wiesner's proposal for a "unilateral moratorium." Wiesner, a member of the National Security Council under Kennedy, suggests that we stop producing more nuclear weapons on our own, then invite the Russians to do the same. If they do, we would reduce our stockpiles by a certain percentage and again invite Moscow to match our effort, until there was complete disarmament.

Simultaneously we would have to disabuse ourselves of the ideological basis for the cold war – mainly, that "you can't trust the Russians." That thesis is irrelevant and obstructive. It is true that we cannot trust the Russian government, but then, we cannot trust *any* government, including our own. Nor should we. Whether we like the Soviet system or not, we and the Soviet people have a common destiny: finding a means of surviving together.

What America needs today is . . . a policy of abolition: we must abolish nuclear weapons. That would not mean scrapping those instruments of death tomorrow morning, but it would mean a *commitment* to do so, and taking certain unilateral initiatives (such as a freeze) while negotiating a quick timetable for abolition.

Reagan was right on one thing. The danger we face is monumental. The sickness is malignant.

"Since 1963, 'The Soviets have had a policy of building forces for a preemptive attack on United States ICBM's.' "

The Soviet Plan

Robert Jastrow

Robert Jastrow was the founder of NASA's Institute for Space Studies and served as its director until his retirement in 1981. He is currently professor of earth sciences at Dartmouth. In the viewpoint that follows, Professor Jastrow presents a case for building more U.S. nuclear weapons in this present age of "overkill". He justifies President Reagan's assessment of American vulnerability by claiming that the country that can blow up the world three times has an advantage over the country that can blow it up only two times.

As you read, consider the following questions:

1. What does MAD refer to? Why does the author claim it is based on a false premise?
2. What does the author claim the Soviet's ultimate plan is?
3. Why does Mr. Jastrow think the arguments against overkill are false? Do you agree?

The policies of the United States for protecting its citizens from destruction are based on a flawed premise.

The premise is that the Soviet Union will be deterred from a surprise nuclear attack on the United States by the knowledge that such an attack would trigger a devastating American counterattack. And, of course, *we* are deterred from an attack on the USSR by the knowledge that the Soviets maintain a similar arsenal. The result is a nuclear standoff, and world peace. . . .

MAD

The academicians who thought up this idea called it Mutual Assured Destruction, or sometimes simply MAD. It makes very good sense, as you would expect, since the policy was formulated by some of the most brilliant scientists and academicians who have ever served in an advisory capacity to our government. The trouble is that MAD is a theory, and like all theories, it depends on an assumption. This assumption has turned out to be false.

The assumption behind the theory of Mutual Assured Destruction is that both the United States and the USSR will freely offer up their populations for massacre. But this requires that each country give up all attempts to defend its own people. In other words, the two countries must agree that neither will have a civil-defense program, and neither side will try to shoot down the other side's missiles. . . .

Actually, MAD is a logical response to the problem of nuclear war, and it could have worked, *if* the Russians had been reasonable and seen matters our way – if they had been willing to offer up their people as hostages, just as we have done. But the Soviet Union saw things differently.

It is now clear – in fact it has been clear for a decade – that while for many years the American government adopted the strategy of Mutual Assured Destruction proposed by our scientists and academicians, the Soviet government rejected it. The USSR undertook to do exactly what our strategists say it is supposed not to do: it implemented large programs for defending its citizens from nuclear attack, for shooting down American missiles, and for fighting and winning a nuclear war. . . .

The Russians have made it clear that they think the theories of the American scientist-advisers are crazy, and they want no part of them. Their rejection goes beyond the concept of Mutual Assured Destruction itself; they reject the view, so widely held in America, that the mass detonation of nuclear weapons would

34

mean the end of civilization, and, therefore, that these weapons are not useful tools of military policy.

The Soviet Plan

At one time, Soviet thinking on nuclear war did echo American ideas on the impossibility of a nuclear victory. That was in the 1950's, soon after Stalin's death, when Malenkov, who was then the Soviet premier, announced that nuclear war could lead to the "destruction of world civilization." But Malenkov was severely criticized by Khrushchev, who said he had it wrong; only capitalism would perish in a nuclear war. By the mid-1960's the debate was over, and the elements of Soviet nuclear policy were set in concrete. In 1979, Secretary of Defense Brown confirmed that since 1963, "The Soviets have had a policy of building forces for a preemptive attack on United States ICBM's."

And in fact Soviet military writings make it plain that the entire war-fighting posture of the Soviet General Staff rests on the mass use of nuclear missiles:

> The most important task of the General Staff in preparing for a modern war is the detailed planning of employment of nuclear weapons by all services of the armed forces.

> The armed forces of the Soviet Union . . . must be prepared above all to wage war under conditions of the mass use of nuclear weapons.

> The basic method of waging war will be massed nuclear rocket attack. . . .

> Nuclear missile strikes . . . and the ability to use them before the opponent does, are the key to victory.

> It is recommended that the nuclear strike be launched . . . unexpectedly for the enemy. Preemption in launching a nuclear strike is expected to be the decisive condition for the attainment of superiority.

The Soviet Buildup

Some American scientists and arms-control experts find it hard to believe that the Russians can actually hold these views on the massive use of nuclear weapons. They feel that if the Russian generals think they can fight and win a nuclear war, the reason must be that the generals have not thought the question through carefully. "I don't think we should substitute their judgment for our common sense," said Paul Warnke about the matter. Warnke, who was President Carter's chief arms-control negotiator, thought Russian thinking about emerging victorious from a nuclear war was "primitive," and the United States "ought to educate them into the real world of strategic nuclear weapons."

35

THREADS OF EVIDENCE NOW CONVINCE OFFICIALS THAT INTERNATIONAL TERRORISM, MURDER, KIDNAPPINGS AND BOMBINGS ARE ALL TIED TOGETHER. *NEWS*

SURPRISE

THE UNION LEADER, N.H.

Jim Dobbins, *Manchester Union Leader*. Reprinted with permission.

But the Russians have refused to be educated. Around 1963, in pursuit of their objective of winning a nuclear war if it should break out, they began a massive program for building nuclear bombs, missiles, and submarines. In the next few years, American satellites photographed new missile silos sprouting all over the Soviet Union. In 1967, the Russians built 160 new silos; in 1968, they added 340 more; in 1969, they drew abreast of the United States. By then each side had about 1,000 silos and a like number of missiles.

None of this bothered American strategists because their policy of Mutual Assured Destruction required that each country must have enough nuclear destructive power to kill a lot of the other fellows. Secretary of Defense Robert McNamara had figured out that we had enough bombs to kill at least 50 million Russians directly in a mass nuclear attack, in addition to millions who would die later from radiation poisoning. He stated that he thought this was sufficient to deter the Russians from starting anything. Therefore, in 1967, he froze the United States force of ICBM's at 1,000 Minutemen plus 54 of the older Titans. He also

froze the number of missiles carried by our nuclear submarines at 656. Secretary McNamara had said a few years earlier: "There is no indication that the Soviets are seeking to develop a strategic nuclear force as large as our own." The Secretary was relaxed about the Soviet build-up; his feeling was that if the Soviets improved their capabilities for blowing us up, they could be more equal partners in the strategy of Mutual Assured Destruction, and the peace of the world would be more secure.

So, while the Russians were working away at increasing the size of their nuclear arsenal, the United States made no attempt to stay ahead of them, and the number of American missiles and nuclear submarines remained fixed at their 1967 levels. Meanwhile the Soviet military budget continued to climb. It went up steadily, 4 percent a year, year after year. At the same time, the American defense budget, exclusive of Vietnam, began to decline. In 1970, the two budgets crossed – one going up, and the other going down. Still the Soviet budget continued to increase, especially in the area of strategic forces – nuclear bombs, missiles, and submarines – where the Soviets spent about $40 billion a year, while American expenditures in this critical area of defense averaged about $12 billion a year.

By 1969 or 1970, the effects of the massive Soviet build-up were becoming apparent. In round numbers, the Soviet Union now had 1,400 ICBM's plus another 300 nuclear missiles in submarines. Meanwhile, the U.S. strategic forces remained frozen at their 1967 levels of 1,054 ICBM's and 656 nuclear-submarine missiles. Soviet superiority in ICBM's was roughly balanced by our edge in submarine-launched missiles. (We still had a fleet of aging B-52 bombers, but their usefulness against the massive Soviet air defenses was open to question.) Overall the Russians were about equal to us in nuclear destructive power.

Now both sides met the requirements for Mutual Assured Destruction. Each possessed enough weapons to inflict serious damage on the other fellow, and to American strategists, any further build-up by either nation would have been pointless. All that remained was to sit down with the Russians and formalize the arrangement with an arms-control treaty. SALT – the Strategic Arms Limitation Talks – was the result.

Soviets Cheat on SALT

SALT, ratified in 1972, did not actually limit the number of nuclear bombs in the American and Russian arsenals. What it limited was objects that carry bombs, such as missile silos and nuclear submarines. A missile silo, as Senator Moynihan has

pointed out, is a hole in the ground, and it can hurt you if you fall into it, but otherwise it is harmless. A true arms-control treaty should have limited the number and size of the nuclear weapons in the arsenals of the two countries. But the United States was never able to get the Soviet Union to agree to anything like that; the Russians would only accept a limit on items such as the number of holes in the ground.

Even so, the Russians found it difficult to live by the terms of the treaty after they signed it. Some years ago, for example, our satellites caught them in the act of digging 150 extra missile silos that were not permitted by the SALT treaty. When the United States brought this matter to the attention of the Russians, they explained that the new holes were launch-control silos, intended to house the crews and equipment which launched the missiles. But the extra silos had special doors of the kind that pop open to permit a missile's quick escape. A silo with a pop-up door is essential for launching missiles, but highly undesirable for housing the launch-control crew, which usually is housed in an underground bunker to protect it from radiation and other effects of nuclear attack. Whatever use the additional silos might be put to initially, it was obvious that they were meant to be convertible to missile silos at a moment's notice.

Specialists monitoring Soviet compliance with the SALT treaty have reported many other violations. Some are ominous because they indicate a serious intent to deceive the United States. . . .

Overkill, Another False Assumption

But does it matter? As Secretary of State Henry Kissinger once asked: "What in the name of God is strategic superiority? . . . What do you do with it?" The American strategic-nuclear arsenal, divided into the population of the world, is equivalent to a half ton of TNT per person. The Soviet strategic-nuclear arsenal is equivalent to two tons of TNT per person. Nothing seems to demonstrate the folly of building additional bombs and missiles more clearly than these numbers. By any reasonable criterion, both the United States and the Soviet Union have acquired "overkill."

But the reasoning that leads to the idea of overkill, like the reasoning that leads to Mutual Assured Destruction, is based on an assumption. This assumption, again, has turned out to be false. The assumption is that the bombs of the Russians and of the Americans will be exploded over cities. This is what is meant

by holding the civilian population hostage. The Russians, however, have made it plain that they find no merit in this idea. In their planning, the top-priority targets are not our cities but our missile silos, bombers, and submarines – and the communication links which would carry the orders for attack to their commanders. In other words, the Soviets aim to prevent us – in the event war should break out – from inflicting damage on their country.

How would the Soviet Union accomplish that objective? Civilian defense, air defense, and missile defense are part of the answer, and the Soviets have large programs in each of those areas. Civil defense is a fifth arm of the Soviet military, with status equal to that of the Soviet Strategic Rocket Forces, Air Force, Army, and Navy.

Another part of the answer is the 5,000 warheads on Soviet ICBM's. It is true that a small fraction of that huge arsenal could destroy every major city in the United States, but the warheads are not intended for that purpose; they are targeted against our 1,054 missile silos, probably two to a silo. This redundancy will insure nearly complete destruction of the American missile force, even when allowance is made for the fact that some Soviet missiles will not get off the ground, others will wander off course, and some will fail to explode.

Thus, the targeted American missile force accounts for approximately 2,000 of the 5,000 Soviet ICBM warheads. Another 500 warheads could be targeted on military airfields and whatever nuclear-missile submarines are in port or can be located. An additional 500 warheads could be allotted to the destruction of our military command-and-control centers and our military-communication links, with the aim of compromising the system by which instructions flow from the President and senior officials to military commanders in the field for the launch of a retaliatory strike on the Soviet Union.

This would leave a force of 2,000 ICBM warheads still available to the Soviet Union for use in deterring the United States from launching a retaliatory second strike with the ICBM's, bombers, or submarine missiles that had survived the first strike. If our government failed to see the wisdom of submission at this stage, and launched a retaliatory strike against Soviet cities, Russian reprisal would be swift and devastating, and the life of our nation would be ended.

What about our nuclear submarines? A great many Americans feel that submarines will be the ultimate deterrent to Soviet attack, regardless of the number of ICBM's in the Soviet arsenal.

American Trident submarines are nearly invulnerable to detection when at sea, and, as President Carter once pointed out, the nuclear warheads carried on a single one of these would be sufficient to destroy all the largest cities in the Soviet Union.

The difficulty with this line of thinking is that missiles launched from submarines can only be used to attack cities and similar "soft" targets. The reason is that a submarine never knows precisely where it is in the ocean. Although the path of the submarine-launched missile may be very accurately guided during its flight, if the starting point of the missile's trajectory is uncertain, the place where it lands must be equally uncertain. As a consequence, the accuracy of submarine-launched missiles is relatively poor.

American submarines and their missiles therefore cannot be used to eliminate the missile force of the Soviet Union, or its command-and-control centers, because those targets, hardened with reinforced concrete and underground construction, can be destroyed only by the pinpoint accuracy of a direct hit. (An attack on cities does not require great accuracy, since the power of the nuclear weapon will destroy a city if the bomb explodes anywhere in the vicinity.)

These considerations indicate why American submarines cannot substitute for our force of Minutemen, as a deterrent to Soviet attack. From the limited accuracy of submarine-launched missiles it follows that these missiles can only be used against cities. Therefore they cannot be used at all, because our government will know that if used in this way, they will trigger a punishing Soviet counterattack on our own cities. What President would decide to launch our submarine missiles in an attack on Leningrad and Moscow, knowing that New York and Washington would be destroyed in return? Faced with this option, any government would prefer to live and fight another day.

Conclusion

In the course of time, technology will improve the accuracy of our submarine-launched nuclear missiles to the point where they will have a hard-target "kill" capability, and the American deterrent will be restored. According to present estimates, that should happen by the end of the 1980's. The intervening four to five years will be, as Dr. Kissinger has said, "a period of vulnerability such as we have not experienced since the early days of the Republic."

If the nuclear-freeze movement is successful, the period of

vulnerability will be extended into the 1990's. Assuming that does not happen, how will the Russians make use of the four to five years of nuclear superiority they will still enjoy? . . .

When will the Russians make their move? Leonid Brezhnev supplied the timetable a few years ago, in a speech to Community leaders in Prague:

> We are achieving with detente what our predecessors have been unable to achieve using the fist. . . . By 1985, . . . we will have achieved most of our objectives in Western Europe. . . . Come 1985, we will be able to extend our will wherever we need to. . . .

And so we finally see why strategic superiority matters. We see how it is that, as Senator Moynihan has said, he who can blow the world up three times has more power than he who can blow it up only twice.

"The Russians are not coming, folks, so keep your shirts on . . . . The fundamental truth, in fact, is that they are weak, and getting weaker, and we are strong."

The Russians Are Not Coming

William Greider

William Greider was assistant managing editor and a columnist for the *Washington Post*. He is now national editor of *Rolling Stone*. Mr. Greider claims American reaction to the Soviet threat is unwarranted and borders on hysteria. In the following viewpoint, excerpted from Mr. Greider's essay in the anthology *Waging Peace*, the author states America is not vulnerable. Mr. Greider argues that anyone of normal intelligence who examines the balance of power will quickly conclude that while America is strong and getting stronger, the Soviets are growing weaker.

As you read, consider the following questions:

1. Why does the author think the Russian threat to Western Europe is overstated?
2. What two "flimsy assumptions" does the author claim the window of vulnerability concept is based on?
3. What evidence does the author present to support his claim that the Soviet Union is in deep trouble?

William Greider, "Hysteria Is Coming, Hysteria Is Coming," *The Washington Post*, September 28, 1980. Reprinted with permission.

I don't blame ordinary citizens for ignorance in this matter of the Red Menace. . . . Life is too short to spend it reading *Foreign Affairs* and the other turgid journals where the Cold War is fought out in dense, bloodless theory. Normal people have better things to do.

I do blame ordinary citizens, though, for being so easily seduced by the new hysteria over national defense, a collective obsession . . . that is going to prove outrageously expensive and, if God isn't looking out for us, dangerous.

If Americans kept closer tab of their history, they would remember that they have been duped before by the cold warriors, stampeded by apocalyptic warnings that proved false. The Russians are coming. The Reds are superior. We are vulnerable. Armageddon is just around the corner. Unless, of course, we spend a trillion dollars. Yes, we intend to spend a trillion dollars on defense in the next five years.

We Are Not Vulnerable

Well, the Russians are not coming, folks, so keep your shirts on (if you have them left). The fundamental truth, in fact, is that *they* are weak, and getting weaker, and we are strong. We are not vulnerable. In the present season of martial music, that assertion marks one as irresponsible or, worse, craven. But I am confident that history is on my side.

A few years hence, I predict, the same learned theoreticians who are now exciting national fears will be writing thoughtful articles about how we misinterpreted and overestimated to produce the born-again Cold War of 1980. Perhaps they will make discreet comparisons with the "missile gap" of 1960 when a similar hysteria aroused by some of the same experts proved phoney. Except that is resulted in the very real arms buildup of the '60s.

Many Americans seem intimidated by this Cold War priesthood. They needn't be. Anyone of normal intelligence who can understand the strategies and imponderables of pro football on Sunday afternoon can easily grasp the basics of the national security debates. Cold War theories are crude bits of whimsy compared with the thoroughgoing war games of a Tom Landry or George Allen.

The difference is this: Those football coaches must test their game plans every Sunday afternoon. The nuclear thinkers have been indulged by history, never tested by the real thing, never forced to discover what a nuclear exchange would really be like. This should tell us something about how much theory to believe,

for in the history of human warfare, particularly in the 20th century, new weapons have always altered warmaking in horrible new ways that were not predicted beforehand. Consider the machine gun in World War I or aerial bombing in World War II.

Anyone of Normal Intelligence
Can Understand National Security

If any earnest citizen wants to understand, the relevant information is not top secret. Much of it has been printed in your daily newspaper. But first one has to cut through the general noise of alarm bells and define the three different arguments contained in this new wave of fright (next, one can go to the public library and read a few old articles, all written in plain English).

"The Russians have us outnumbered in tanks and troops and planes – they could sweep across the Rhine and reach the English Channel in a matter of days and we wouldn't be able to stop them."

This is the favorite spectre invoked by those arguing for a big buildup in conventional arms. Sometimes, these days, they substitute the Midwest for Western Europe. The argument regularly invokes deceitful comparisons – our tanks vs. their tanks – which even the densest senator must know is a phoney numbers game.

The U.S. military opted for the best and most expensive model of virtually every weapons system, including antitank wizardry; the Russian tank is crude and simple compared with our million-dollar electronic marvels. The Soviets, out of their own necessities, build on the cheap and build many more. Nobody, as far as I know, is seriously proposing to change our development strategy or even to match the Russians tank-for-tank, plane-for-plane. Yet they still play the numbers game because it sounds so scary.

A reasonable question about the crossing-the-Rhine scenario is why the Europeans, who would be the immediate victims, are less alarmed than we seem to be. Indeed, a reasonable citizen might ask: If we are headed toward disaster, why are our allies spending so much less on defense than we are?

One reason might be that nobody seriously believes the Russians are planning such an offensive or that they could pull it off without starting World War III, last in a series. The crossing-the-Rhine theories presume or pretend that neither the United States nor our allies would respond with the big one: nuclear

weapons. We are pledged to do so. It would be a rather desperate gamble for the Soviet leaders to roll the dice and find out if we meant it.

But why then do the Russians have all those tanks in Eastern Europe, if not to threaten us? Recent headlines provided one of the main answers: to threaten their own satellites and keep them in line.

The Vulnerability Myth

U.S. conventional forces do have serious and costly problems: the replacement of worn-out equipment, inadequate maintenance, the technological escalation of weapons and their soaring price tags, the shortage of pilots and experienced technicians in the ranks. But none of these problems is a function of Soviet hegemony; none will be solved by scaring folks.

"For the next four or five years, the United States is in a dangerous window of vulnerability – the Soviet Union could start a nuclear war and win it."

This is the notion that launched the $80 billion MX missile "racetrack" scheme, a proposal so dubious that even some conservative hawks oppose it. The fear is that the Soviets now have enough megatonnage in place, ready to fire, to knock out all our land-based missiles in one strike. Though this is theoretically

Don Wright, *Miami News.* Reprinted with permission.

true, no one should be surprised by the development; the Soviets have been building toward nuclear parity with us for the last decade. Anyway, the "window of vulnerability" theory depends on two very flimsy assumptions.

First, that the Soviet leaders, in some sort of crazy desperation, must be prepared for 100 million dead Russians if their gamble is wrong. This is what's known as "war-winning capability." The Soviet leaders are a brutish, hostile lot, but I don't believe they define 100 million dead comrades as victory.

Second, that the U.S. president will surrender without a fight. Our land-based missiles are destroyed, tens of millions of Americans have been killed, radiation death is spreading across our land, but the president decides not to retaliate with our thousands of protected bombs on submarines and bombers. Why? By the logic of vulnerability, he would conclude that it wasn't worth it, that more lives would be lost, ours and theirs, and we would wind up in total devastation. A humanitarian view.

Do you believe that? Nothing in American history suggests a precedent for surrender. Indeed, the history of modern warfare, in which many nations have faced similar choices, is filled with eloquent stories of leaders and peoples between devastation and surrender who chose terrible suffering before defeat and subjugation. Would Americans somehow be different?

The "vulnerability" issue evades the larger and now-permanent reality: Both sides have overabundant nuclear arsenals, sufficiently protected from attack, to obliterate the other after absorbing a first strike, if necessary. Together, by 1985, we will have more than 35,000 warheads; we already have 14 billion tons of exposives, three tons each for every living mortal.

"We're not really talking about actual strengths and weaknesses – we're talking about the perception of weakness. If it looks like Russia's arsenal is bigger than ours, it will influence world politics. Therefore, build we must."

This "perception of weakness" is the core anxiety, I believe, a spiritual malaise which infected cold warriors at the fall of Saigon. The argument is really a kind of self-fulfilling theology which lies beyond proof. To prevent the "perception of weakness," we should commit a fixed percentage of our growing national wealth to the military and argue later about how to spend it. This is roughly what the government is now trying to do, and it resembles the primitive rite of offering sacrifice at the altar of the war god.

46

The Soviet Union Is In Deep Trouble

What's more scandalous is this: The so-called "perception of weakness" is fundamentally wrong. The Soviet Union, as every scholar knows, is in deep trouble, at home and abroad, in the long run and in the immediate future. The scary image of Soviet hegemony, so familiar to American consumers, simply doesn't fit the facts.

The popular rebellion in Poland. The quagmire in Afghanistan. The Islamic reformation, which is much more threatening to the USSR than to us because a growing portion of the Soviet population is Moslem. The new tactical nukes in Germany which threaten from the West. And, from the East, the new U.S. alliance with China.

The list goes on. While Americans never seem to see these as ominous for the Soviet leaders, the Soviet leaders do. Their perception is almost a perfect reverse mirror of the U.S. cold warriors' perception: The Soviets see themselves encircled, threatened, endangered.

The long-run outlook for the Russians is even worse. The basic problem, after all the ideological rhetoric has been brushed aside, is simple: Their system doesn't work. The Soviet economy can't grow fast enough to buy all the military hardware and, at the same time, provide elementary consumer goods. It has to buy food from America. It has to borrow technology. Satellite nations like Poland have to borrow capital from Western bankers to stay afloat. Still, the Polish workers go on strike. That's why all those Russian tanks are in Eastern Europe.

These historic contradictions will become more intense in the 1980s because the Soviet population is changing in adverse ways. Because of abortions, a rising rate of infant mortality, and a declining birth rate, the age group of young workers is shrinking as a proportion of society – and shifting, incidentally, away from the urban centers of industry and toward provincial minorities like the Moslems. None of this is expected to undo Lenin's revolution. But, at the very least, the Commies are facing hard times that make our difficulties seem benign and manageable.

Everything I have said here has been said before, has been printed in newspapers and articles. Yet I would guess that much of it will be news to ordinary Americans. They don't pay close attention to the undramatic and tedious details, but they sit up and listen when someone cries "war."

I don't blame them for selective inattention, but I do think

this: If Americans don't get smarter about themselves and the world, someday they are going to get hurt by what they don't know.

"The most important social service a government can do for its people is to keep them alive and free."

Military Strength Insures Freedom

Caspar W. Weinberger

Caspar W. Weinberger is Secretary of Defense in the Reagan Administration. He has held a number of key positions in government, including Secretary of Health, Education, and Welfare from 1973 to 1975. Secretary Weinberger is a strong advocate of increased defense spending. The following viewpoint is excerpted from *Defense* magazine, a publication of the Department of Defense (DOD) to provide official information to DOD personnel. In it, Mr. Weinberger argues for increased military spending, claiming that money spent on defense is the best investment America can make.

As you read, consider the following questions:

1. What does Secretary Weinberger claim are the three important tenets for maintaining national security?
2. How does Secretary Weinberger respond to those who "contend we cannot fund adequate levels of defense because funds are needed elsewhere"?
3. Why does the author think we should modernize our nuclear capability and maintain planned defense expenditures for several years? Do you agree?

Caspar Weinberger, "Seeking Consensus for the Common Defense," *Defense* Magazine, December 1982.

One of the greatest challenges in defending a free society rests in our democratic principles which require a consensus to be formed in favor of a strong defense, if we are to have one, and for that consensus continually to be maintained. This task has never been easy in open democratic societies.

From the earliest days of our republic we have loved peace and been suspicious of things military. Within six months of the end of the Revolutionary War, the Continental Congress, believing that "standing armies in time of peace are inconsistent with principles of republican Government" and "are dangerous to the liberties of a free people," disbanded the remnant of the Continental Army, reducing the number of troops from 700 regulars to 25 privates to guard the stores at Fort Pitt and 55 to guard the stores at West Point. No officer was permitted to remain in service above the rank of captain.

Later, during the debates on the Constitution, a clause was offered that would have prohibited our new Armed Forces from exceeding 3,000 men. Washington said he would support the proposal if the author would accept an amendment that prohibited any invading Army from exceeding 2,000.

Today, the Reagan Administration is striving to maintain a consensus for national security. This consensus has three important and mutually supportive tenets:

First: *We will sustain adequate levels of defense strength – this requires time and money;*
Second: *We will honor commitments to our allies;*
Third: *We will pursue effective arms reduction agreements.*

Because each of these tenets is important, I would like to discuss them in some detail.

Strengthening Our Defenses

First, the Reagan Administration is committed to strengthening the defenses necessary to deter any attack on us. In times of severe budgetary constraints, this is a painful commitment which has often produced conflict.

Walter Lippmann once wrote, "In my youth, we all assumed that the money spent on battleships would be better spent on schoolhouses." This is a sympathetic theme and one that is reinforced by the paradox that if we, in the defense of our country, completely succeed in what we are doing, we will never have to use any of these weapons we must acquire.

The resources devoted to defense, if spent for other things,

could accomplish considerable public good. But we must not forget that "the most important social service a government can do for its people is to keep them alive and free." This is an obligation we have been dangerously close to neglecting.

Apart from the Vietnam era, United States defense spending, in constant dollars, remained virtually unchanged from the mid-1950s through the end of the 1970s. Moreover, relative to Gross National Product, our defense effort dropped dramatically, declining from 8.3 percent of Gross National Product in 1960 to 4.9 percent in 1979. The share of defense activity in the Federal Budget also shrank by nearly one-half, falling from over 45 percent in 1960 to less than 25 percent in 1979.

In the post-Vietnam era, we overlooked critically needed modernization requirements and permitted decay in the readiness of our forces. At the same time, the Soviet Union was greatly increasing expenditures for defense. As a result, we found ourselves in 1980 in a considerably weaker position than we had been in any period since World War II. . . .

To those who contend that we cannot fund adequate levels of defense because funds are needed elsewhere, I can only reply that they are making the wrong calculations. Expenditures for

Negotiating position

Reprinted by permission of United Features Syndicate.

defense cannot be determined by what is left over from other programs – rather, they must be measured against the threat we actually face.

That threat is very real today, and it is a growing threat. James Madison said: "The means of security can only be regulated by the means and the danger of attack. . . . If one nation maintains constantly a disciplined Army, ready for the service of ambition or revenge, it obliges the most pacific nations, who may be within the reach of its enterprises, to take corresponding precautions."

Honoring Our Commitments

The *second* way we can protect the nation is by honoring commitments to our allies. This is also an idea with a checkered history. From Washington's warning against entangling alliances to modern proposals advocating withdrawal of our troops from Europe, our nation has possessed a strong strain of isolationism. But the period in which this isolationism could be supported by the natural barriers of our geography has long since passed.

No longer can we delude ourselves that commitments to our allies spring only from an altruistic desire to preserve their freedom. In fact – defense of their freedom is simply the forward defense of our own freedom.

In 1935, Phillip Jessup speculated, "It may not be many years before it·is alleged that the air frontiers of the United States are on the far sides of the Atlantic and Pacific Oceans." Mr. Jessup. lived to see his prophecy fulfilled. It is clear that we could not survive for long in the world if Europe is overrun.

Despite this reality, there are some today who are critical of our commitment to our allies, particularly those who seek a lessening of this Administration's deep commitment to NATO.

NATO, as one of the most successful alliances in world history, has assured Europe the longest period of peace in modern history. Its vitality has been reinforced recently by the entry of Spain. Because it has been so effective, it has been a cardinal point of Soviet strategy to try to destroy the Alliance. There is also a temptation to take NATO's benefits for granted and for some to wonder if the Alliance is worth the effort. This leads to talk of inequitable burdensharing, particularly during periods of budgetary strain.

We cannot let such strains obscure the very real contributions of our allies to their own defense and to the defense of other nations. . . .

Pursuing Arms Reductions

The *third* tenet of our security consensus is the pursuit of effective arms reduction agreements. Early in the Administration, we decided that the very best way to achieve lasting peace with the Soviets would be to persuade them to agree to major, verifiable arms reductions, down to equality on both sides at vastly lower levels than we now have.

The United States has put forward a comprehensive arms reduction program which includes the elimination of land-based intermediate range missiles, a one-third reduction in strategic ballistic missile warheads, a substantial reduction in NATO and Warsaw Pact ground and air forces, and new safeguards to reduce the risk of accidental war. However, we have not pursued this process blindly; we have established four essential criteria by which we will evaluate any arms reduction proposals.

1. We insist on significant reductions. We are committed to reducing the number and destructive potential of weapons, not just freezing them at high levels or authorizing even higher levels, as we did in previous SALT agreements.

2. We seek equality and will accept nothing less. We want agreements that will lead to mutual reductions down to equal levels of effective forces on both sides. We believe that this equality is aboslutely necessary if we are to provide our country with adequate security. In measuring this equality, we will focus on the destructive power of weapons – not just on such considerations as numbers of launchers. A launcher by itself has no destructive power, yet that was the measure used in SALT II. It was of course agreed to, indeed proposed by, the Soviets because it enabled them to continue, as they are to this very hour, to acquire more, heavier, and more accurate lethal weapons.

3. We will insist on verifiability. The United States will draft carefully the provisions of arms control agreements and insist on measures to ensure compliance by both sides. I am sure you can appreciate the absolute necessity of this requirement.

Indeed, we have very good evidence that the Soviet Union has broken their "no first use of chemical weapons" agreement. Moreover, certain Soviet tests have been of sufficient magnitude to raise serious questions about compliance with the 150 kiloton limit of the Threshold Test Ban Treaty. These two points indicate the need for improved verification procedures. In this connection, it is significant that we have always offered full on-site verification, and we still do.

We are yet a long way from Grenville Clark's Utopia where

there is World Peace through World Law. In the world in which we presently live, arms reduction agreements provide no security without agreement on adequate and effective verification.

4. *We will insist that arms control agreements genuinely enhance United States and allied security.* We must not accept cosmetic agreements that lull the public into a false sense of security. As lawyers, we know that, while it may be easier to reach an agreement for a client if difficult issues are ignored or purposely blurred, in the long run, we have done our client no service. We will not fall into this trap.

We do not seek arms agreements for agreements' sake, but rather to enhance our national security and reduce the risk of nuclear war. Some feel that if we enter into negotiations, the end result must be an agreement, even if it is not a good agreement for us. I am afraid some of that reasoning permeated the SALT negotiations.

Soviet and US Arms Deliveries
To the Third World
(1977-1981)

	USSR	US
Tanks	7,000	3,000
Artillery	10,000	3,000
Combat Aircraft	3,000	1,000
Surface-To-Air Missiles	12,000	8,000
Helicopters	1,000	2000

Source: *Conventional Arms Transfers in the Third World, 1972-81.* August 1982, US Department of State. (All numbers rounded.)

The prospect of nuclear war is of course thoroughly and totally abhorrent to all of us. The specter of carnage, death, and destruction which such a war or indeed any war would produce is indeed terrifying. Our shared fear of nuclear war has motivated some to advocate proposals which, while wellmeaning, pose a serious threat to our ability to negotiate effective arms control agreements. These include the "nuclear freeze" and "no first use" proposals.

Advocates of a nuclear freeze believe arms control negotiations would more likely be successful if we declared in advance of the successful completion of these negotiations a willingness to

freeze our nuclear capabilities at present levels. This approach has several dangers. It places no concurrent restraints on the Soviet Union which is almost daily improving and increasing its nuclear capabilities. . . .

There is another danger of the freeze proposal. By weakening our resolve to strengthen our nuclear defense, advocates of the freeze would virtually destroy our ability to negotiate genuine arms reductions. As lawyers, we know that our ability to negotiate a settlement before trial is dependent on the strength of our case and the willingness of our clients to go to trial if necessary. How many of us would voluntarily announce our intentions not to engage in discovery, or prepare for trial with the expectation that by thus restraining ourselves we could secure a better settlement? The notion is preposterous. Though discovery and trial preparation are time-consuming and expensive, we would be guilty of the grossest malpractice if we did not continue to prepare vigorously for trial, even though we may hope and even expect that a fair settlement is possible.

By the same token, we must continue to show our resolve to modernize our nuclear capability, even though we of course earnestly hope to negotiate major and effective arms reduction agreements. Only by maintaining our strength can we produce the pressure necessary to get the Soviets to agree to advantageous arms reduction agreements.

Furthermore, only by continuing to modernize our capabilities, while seeking fair arms reduction agreements, will we be adequately safeguarded, if negotiations should not be successful. Nuclear deterrence may be an unpopular notion, but there is no refuting the fact that it has worked. And just think for the moment of the alternatives – a military strength too weak to deter.

It is no good uttering the banal cliche that each superpower has enough to blow each other up. We must do a more thorough analysis than that, and when we do, we see that the Soviets have greatly increased the accuracy and the yield of their missiles, and their ability to withstand retaliatory strikes – while we have not. We have had enough deterrent strength in the past – enough to prevent nuclear war and also to prevent conventional war between the superpowers. We cannot abandon this crucial element of our security until it has been replaced by effective and verifiable arms reduction agreements, and the margin for error here is exceedingly small.

"No first use" proposals pose a different threat to our security by removing an important element necessary to deter the Soviet

Union from use of their tremendous conventional capability. I already have alluded to the astonishing growth of the Soviets' conventional capability which far exceeds their requirements for defense and indeed represents enormous offensive potential.

Those calling for a declaration of "No first use of nuclear weapons" by the United States have forgotten that we already have a No First Use Policy involving all our weapons – conventional or nuclear. Our weapons are intended for defense alone. We will not employ them unless necessary to preserve our peace and security. But to declare a policy of no first use of nuclear weapons is an open invitation to the Soviet Union to use their conventional strength to threaten us and our allies.

We must remember that, while the destructive power of nuclear weapons is awesome, conventional weapons also have the capacity to intimidate and to destroy all that we value. Until we negotiate real arms reduction agreements and are confident of our ability to provide a creditable conventional deterrent, we must not limit our ability to provide a flexible response to aggression.

Conclusion

These, then, are the important elements of a strong defense which the Reagan Administration seeks to maintain: adequate rearmament in time; firm commitment to our allies; and vigorous pursuit of effective arms reduction. Each of these elements is mutually supportive. We must maintain adequate levels of defense expenditures for several years to enable us to meet our commitments to our allies and to provide incentives for arms reduction.

Our commitments to our allies enhance the effective use of our own resources and provide additional incentives for arms reduction.

Meaningful, verifiable arms reductions can lead to major reductions in defense expenditures and also enhance our ability to meet commitments to our allies.

Although each element of this Triad is important, in some measure each is subject to attack by those who do not understand the full extent of our security needs.

"The bulk of the US military budget (80%) goes into 'power projection' forces to distant places, while only 20% goes for the actual defense of the US continent."

U.S. Forces
Foster Exploitation

American Friends Service Committee

The American Friends Service Committee (AFSC) was founded in 1917 to speak out and work against war. It is dedicated to nonviolence and grew out of the Society of Friends, a Quaker movement. The following viewpoint is excerpted from an AFSC booklet, *Questions & Answers On the Soviet Threat and National Security*. AFSC claims that American military forces are used primarily to extend American influence abroad and that the Soviet threat is a convenient excuse to support repressive regimes around the world.

As you read, consider the following questions:

1. Why does this viewpoint claim that U.S. nuclear armaments make Americans less secure?
2. What evidence is presented to support the viewpoint's claim that American military and economic commitments overseas undermine freedom and democracy?

American Friends Service Committee Disarmament Program, "Questions and Answers on the Soviet Threat and National Security," fifth printing, March 1982.

We do have to provide for national security. A strong military makes us secure, doesn't it?

In the short run, arms may make people feel secure. The problem is that our reliance on nuclear armaments which appears to increase security actually is making us less and less secure. Each day, the United States adds 3 new nuclear warheads to its stockpile of over 9,200 strategic nuclear warheads[1], enough to destroy every Soviet city of 100,000 or more 35 times.[2] Just one of the US's 31 Poseidon submarines carries more explosive power than was detonated in all of Europe and Japan in World War II.[3]

In an attempt to catch up with the US, which has led the nuclear arms race from the start, the Soviet Union is steadily increasing its military power and for the first time, is considered equal to the US in overall strategic nuclear capability.[4] With its present stockpile of 6,000 strategic nuclear warheads,[5] the USSR can destroy every American city of 100,000 or more 28 times.[6] Furthermore, there are already other nations with nuclear weapons, and by 1985, there may be as many as 35 more.[7]

With each escalation of the nuclear arms race our security is actually diminished. Does anyone doubt that we and the Soviets are less secure now than we were in 1945 before nuclear weapons existed? We all experience, almost on a daily basis, a growth in our fears and in our sense that we no longer control our own national destiny or our ability to decide on whether there will be war or peace.

Without a strong defense wouldn't we be vulnerable to attack and invasion as we were in the early days of World War II?

The situation today is totally different than in World War II. There is no real defense against attack by nuclear weapons. It takes 30 minutes or less for a nuclear weapon to travel between the United States and the Soviet Union. The smallest nuclear bomb in either arsenal is three times the size of the bomb that we dropped on Hiroshima.

Nuclear war is a wholly new kind of war. There would be no winners. In a major nuclear exchange, the US would lose over 165 million people and the Soviet Union almost as many.[8] A so-called limited war could kill as many as 20 million in each nation.[9] There can be no quantitative comparison of this kind of war with any in the past.

But if we don't maintain a strong nuclear deterrent, couldn't the Soviets put us in a position where, if we didn't capitulate to their demands, they'd strike first, wipe out our forces and take over?

The "capitulation scenario" has serious flaws. One is the misconception that the US does not already have a strong deterrent.

Just two submarines using their destructive power equal to 1,000 Hiroshima-sized weapons can destroy all the 200 major Soviet cities. In the 1960's Robert McNamara, then Secretary of Defense, demonstrated that 400 nuclear missiles would be an adequate deterrent, since they would be able to destroy 30% of the population and 75% of the industrial capacity of the USSR.[10] So it is virtually impossible that the Soviet Union could ever wipe out our forces without getting wiped out in return. The more important and more difficult question for Americans and Russians is whether our goal should be to threaten each other with mass destruction.

This is exactly the reason that a new alternative to "capitulation" vs. "first strike" must be developed. Instead of a new weapons system (which would surely provoke an equivalent system on the other side) we need to build a security system so that those two unacceptable choices are gradually replaced by a conflict resolution process which, as Robert Johansen writes, can "allow us to avoid war . . . without fear of being bullied or conquered in a world of sometimes selfish and brutal governments."[11] . . .

Doesn't the US have a responsibility to defend freedom and support our allies around the world?

Certainly "defending freedom" and "standing by our friends" are principles that most Americans support. Moreover, most Americans recognize that the US is deeply involved in world affairs: politically, economically, socially and culturally. Like it or not, the US cannot become "isolationist" again. The debate begins over what "freedom" and what "friends" our government defends. Frequently, our "national interests" turn out to be the economic interest of the few.

The US has military pacts with 42 countries and treaties, executive agreements, arms sales, military associations and alliances with 92 countries.[12] The US has given massive quantities ($176 billion since 1945) in foreign military and economic aid,[13] and sold $13 billion worth of arms to 90 foreign countries in FY '79.[14] This represents 56% of the world's arms trade – more than Russia, France, Britain and China combined.

Many Americans believe that the US has engaged in such military and economic commitments for the main purpose of preserving freedom and democracy. But the reality is that the top ten recipients of US military and economic aid, according to Amnesty

International, are also the world's top ten dictatorships or violators of human rights: South Korea, The Philippines, Indonesia, Thailand, Chile, Argentina, Uruguay, Haiti, Brazil and formerly, Iran.[15] Is there any way to justify US support to these governments as "defending freedom"? According to testimony by Senator Alan Cranston (D-CA), 51 countries or 69% of the nations receiving military grants from the US are classified as "repressive regimes". These governments allow US air and naval bases on their soil and offer a "favorable investment climate" for the US multinational corporations: low wages, no unions, no strikes, cheap raw materials and no government regulations. All these countries have conditions "favorable" to US business.[16]

Eugene Black, former president of the World Bank and later President Johnson's advisor on Asian development, summed up the advantages of foreign aid to US business, thus:

> The three major benefits are: (1) foreign aid provides a substantial and immediate market for US goods and services; (2) foreign aid stimulates the development of new overseas markets for US companies; (3) foreign aid orients national economies towards a free enterprise system in which US firms can prosper.[17]

The Annual Report presented by our Secretary of Defense every year says that protection of $168 billion worth of US private corporate investments, along with the "free access to" and the "continued flow" of raw materials, is one major assumption behind and purpose for our military forces.[18]

Since mid-century, the US has not been self-sufficient in its raw materials needs. As a matter of fact, a former Secretary of the Navy said that "69 of 72 vital raw materials without which our businesses could not function, are wholly or in part imported into the US."[19] The US, as 6% of the world's population, actually uses 40% of the world's supply of basic commodities and raw materials, mainly acquired from the Third World.[20]

It is for this reason that the bulk of the US military budget (80%) goes into "power projection" forces to distant places, while only 20% goes for the actual defense of the US continent.[21]

Since 1945, according to the Brookings Institute, the US has used military force 215 times to gain political or economic ends.[22] In the name of national security, or the protection of areas of "vital interests," the US has also threatened the use of nuclear weapons 19 times.[23] (Truman and Eisenhower during the Korean War; Kennedy during the Berlin Crisis and the Cuban Missile Crisis; Nixon during the Vietnam War; and most recently, Carter's explicit nuclear threat in his commitment to defend the Persian Gulf oil fields.)

"...An' naturally, the White House welcomes the opportunity to inform the Congress that that there fence ain't there to keep the Blacks in but to keep the Russians out!"

Reprinted with permission from *The Daily World.*

The question for Americans is first, should we continue to "need" all the resources we gather, use and maintain in the Third World by our military might, and second, whether our military forces, or unused nuclear threats, or economic payoffs can "win friends" and protect our interests in the long run?

Since the end of World War II, the Soviet Union and the US have both jockeyed for more favorable positions in the Third World. But neither superpower has been able to use its military to control indigenous movements totally, in for example, Iran (US) or Iraq and Egypt (USSR).

The Soviet presence in the Third World may have less to do with economics, but rather with superpower rivalry. The Soviet Union produces most of its energy sources and minerals it needs from the huge land mass under its direct control. They have few – if any – investments around the globe. As many experts have pointed out, the Soviet military establishment is designed for different purposes than that of the US, with far more of its budget directed toward internal security and defense and virtually no "power projection" forces.[24]

The crisis in Iran and Afghanistan demonstrated the ineffectiveness of military force to resolve what are basically political problems. Military strength could not free the American hostages nor could it prevent the Soviet Union from invading Afghanistan. Both conflicts confirm the increasing need to develop adequate diplomatic and political means of resolving the kinds of problems we are likely to face in the 1980's – as raw materials dwindle and as massive military arsenals make the idea of "being #1" more and more meaningless.

Many people would agree that we need a new foreign policy that recognizes the legitimate rights of indigenous populations and the need for just compensation for extracted raw materials. To ensure friendly, cooperative relations with the Third World, the US should be in favor of, and help build, a strong, non-aligned independent movement, free of superpower intervention. Such a movement will provide the strongest barrier to Soviet moves in the Third World.

1. US Dept. of Defense, *Annual Report for FY 1981,* Harold Brown, Sec. of Defense, Jan. 1, 1979, p. 89.

2. Admiral Gene LaRocque, "Survival: The Most Important Issue of Our Times," *ESA Forum-44,* Washington, DC, p. 25.

3. US Dept. of State Publication 8947, released June, 1978, p. 1.

4. US Dept. of State Publication, "SALT and American Security," released Nov. 1978, p. 3.

5. Same as #1.

6. Same as #2.

7. US Energy, Resources and Development Agency (now DOE), as quoted in *The Defense Monitor,* Center for Defense Information, Feb. 1979; also William Epstein, "The Proliferation of Nuclear Weapons," *Scientific American,* April, 1975.

8. US Office of Technology Assessment Report prepared for the Senate Foreign Relations Committee, as quoted in the *New York Times,* May 1979.

9. Same as #8.

10. US Joint Committee on Defense Production of the Congress Study, "Economic and Social Consequences of Nuclear Attacks on the US," March, 1979, p. 23-24.

11. Robert Johansen, *Toward A Dependable Peace,* Working paper #8, World Order Models Project, Institute For World Order, 1978.

12. US Arms Control and Disarmament Agency, and The Center Defense Information, as quoted by E. Raymond Wilson, "The Arms Race and Human Race," *ESA Forum-27, March 1977, p. 21.*

13. *US Agency for International Development Summary, FY 77 and prior years as quoted by the Campaign for a Democratic Foreign Policy, "US Foreign and Military Policy," ESA Forum-27, March 1977, p. 34.*

14. *The US Dept. of Defense, Annual Report,* FY 81, Harold Brown, Secretary of Defense, Jan. 29, 1980, p. 224.

15. Michael Klare, *Supplying Repression,* Institute for Policy Studies, Washington, DC, p. 8.

16. Testimony of Senator Alan Cranston, before the Senate Foreign Relations Committee, July 24, 1974.

17. Columbia Journal of World Business, Vol. 1, Fall, 1965, p. 23.

18. US Dept. of Defense, *Annual Report for FY '81,* Harold Brown, Secretary of Defense, p. 26.

19. US Secretary of the Navy, speech to the National Security Industrial Association, 1972, as quoted by Richard Barnet, *The Giants,* Simon and Schuster, New York, 1977, p. 123.

20. Richard Barnet, *The Economy of Death,* Atheneum Books, NY, 1970, p. 46.

21. The Boston Study Group, *The Price of Defense,* Times Books, NY, 1979, p. 13. The Boston Study Group is composed of Randall Forsberg, MIT; Phylis Morrison; George Sommaripa; Paul Walker, Harvard.

22. "Study Says US Showed Force 215 Times Since '45," Don Oberdorfer, *Washington Post,* January 3, 1977, quoting from the Brookings Institute Study by Barry Blechman and Stephan Kaplan, authors. Study was funded by DOD Advanced Research Projects Agency.

23. "Study Says Military Force Buys Negotiation Time," Drew Middleton, *New York Times,* Dec. 11, 1978, quoting from "Force Without War," by Blechman and Kaplan of the Brookings Institute.

24. Same as #21, p. 36 and , "The Power Projection Gap," Michael Klare, *the Nation,* June 9, 1979, p. 673.

Distinguishing Between Fact and Opinion

This activity is designed to help develop the basic reading and thinking skill of distinguishing between fact and opinion. Consider the following statement as an example. "Israel has one of the most effective armies in the Middle East." This statement is a fact which no historian, political commentator or diplomat of any nationality would deny. But consider a statement which condemns Israel and its army. "The aggressiveness and imperialistic aims of Israel and its army is the chief cause of tensions in the Middle East." Such a statement is clearly an expressed opinion. The motives attributed to Israeli military policy as carried out by the army of Israel obviously will depend upon one's point of view. A citizen of Israel will view the activities of his/her army from a far different perspective than will a member of the Palestine Liberation Organization.

When investigating controversial issues it is important that one be able to distinguish between statements of fact and statements of opinion.

The following statements are taken from the viewpoints in this chapter. Consider each statement carefully. *Mark O for any statement you feel is an opinion or interpretation of facts. Mark F for any statement you believe is a fact.*

If you are doing this activity as the member of a class or group, compare your answers with those of other class or group members. Be able to defend your answers. You may discover that others will come to different conclusions than you. Listening to the reasons others present for their answers may give you valuable insights in distinguishing between fact and opinion.

If you are reading this book alone, ask others if they agree with your answers. You too will find this interaction very valuable.

O = opinion
F = fact

64

1. The defense policy of the United States is based on a simple premise: The United States does not start fights.

2. Deterrence means simply this: Making sure any adversary who thinks about attacking the United States or our allies or our vital interests concludes that the risks to him outweigh any potential gains.

3. The Soviets, for example, have enough accurate and powerful nuclear weapons to destroy virtually all of our missiles on the ground.

4. During the past decade and a half, the Soviets have built up a massive arsenal of new strategic nuclear weapons – weapons that can strike directly at the United States.

5. The final fact is that the Soviet Union is acquiring what can only be considered an offensive military force.

6. In 1968 the United States had 4,200 strategic nuclear warheads, the Soviets 1,100; today we have 9,300, they have 7,300.

7. Our weapons now have guidance systems such as the MARV and the MARK 12-A, which make them at least twice as accurate as Soviet weapons.

8. No nation in history has ever been encircled with more firepower than the Soviet Union is today.

9. The arms race can be ended only by ending it. That means an immediate freeze without quibbling over the niceties of "verification".

10. The difficulty in making comparisons is that each side has different weapons for different strategies.

11. By weakening our resolve to strengthen our nuclear defense, advocates of the freeze would virtually destroy our ability to negotiate genuine arms reduction.

12. We are lovers of peace – and we must use this love of peace to do all the hard things that must be done if we are to preserve both the peace and the freedoms we properly value so highly.

13. Our present course will lead to nuclear annihilation.

14. America is good. And if America ever ceases to be good, America will cease to be great.

15. For the past three years, under two presidents, the United States has been engaged in an effort to stop the advance of communism in Central America by doing what we do best – by supporting democracy.

Is the U.S. a Militaristic Society?

THE
AMERICAN
MILITARY

"In our culture, war is a deep-down, bone-marrow part of the commonsense view of the nature of things."

War Is a Cultural Habit

John Alexis Crane

The Rev. Dr. John Crane presented the following viewpoint as part of a sermon he preached in Jefferson Unitarian Church, Golden, Colorado. In this viewpoint, he claims that war is a deeply rooted habit of our culture because individuals readily grasp its nature and importance. More importantly, he believes that because of culture, individuals find it easy to feel commitment to and enthusiasm for war.

As you read, consider the following questions:

1. Why does the author think the U.S. and the Soviet Union continue a mutually self destructive arms race?
2. How does the author respond to the claim that Russia is responsible for the arms race?
3. Do you think the author's view of American culture could best be labeled optimistic, pessimistic or realistic?

John Alexis Crane, "Does War Make Sense?" *The Churchman*, November 1981. Reprinted with permission.

If you are less than forty years old, the probability is high that you will die in a nuclear war.

This is not a whimsical conclusion of my own, but the careful, considered judgment of a brilliant scientist, George Kistiakowsky, an advisor to presidents Eisenhower, Kennedy, and Johnson, an active participant in the development of nuclear weapons. Dr. Kistiakowsky, about this time last year, said, "I think that with the kind of political leaders we have in the world . . . nuclear weapons will proliferate . . . that the likelihood for an initial use of nuclear warheads is really quite great between now and the end of this century."

I bring the matter up in order to raise our level of consciousness of the matter. The survival of this country depends on our becoming acutely conscious of the meaning and the threat of nuclear war, and taking the action – making the changes – that will prevent it. If we continue to ignore it, pretend it isn't there, do nothing, the probability is great that our country will cease to exist. That's what nuclear war means: the U.S. and Russia will be wiped out, destroyed. . . .

War Is a Cultural Habit

Does it appear rational or even sane that two nations should persist in a course of action that will lead to mutual extinction? Does it make sense that the U.S. and the Soviet Union have spent, and continue to spend, countless billions of dollars on weapons which will result in mutual, total destruction? What kind of national security is that?

Why in heaven's name do not the U.S. and the Soviet Union take decisive steps to end the threat of nuclear war, to ensure a stable peace, since it is overwhelmingly clear not only that it is in their own self-interest, but that it is necessary for sheer survival?

Broadly speaking, it is owing to the fact that war makes sense to the people of the western world. In our culture, war is a deep-down, bone-marrow part of the commonsense view of the nature of things. It doesn't take any imagination or intelligence or effort to understand war. The most ignorant, unintelligent individual can grasp its nature, meaning, and importance, can feel enthusiasm for it, feel utterly committed to it. We have incredible imagination and creativity in conceiving weapons. We have very little imagination in relation to peace. Our thinking about peace is lame and halting. It is done with little imagination or enthusiasm. It is entered into reluctantly; negotiations are interminable.

Steve Sack, *Minneapolis Star & Tribune*. Reprinted with permission.

The U.S. and Russia do not do at all well at making peace because war is a deeply-rooted cultural habit, and it ties in nicely with the fear and hostility we feel toward those we perceive as enemies. People in each nation learn to ignore the facts about

themselves and come to have a distorted, cosmetic understanding. Each nation alters the facts about itself in order to make possible unconditional positive regard. This is not done by conscious, deliberate conspiracy. It's almost a reflex. People do it without thinking. They are not aware of what they are doing.

The answer to the problem of war is to raise their level of awareness, to enable them to be conscious of the reality of their nation rather than its beautiful image. The prevailing view in our mass media and of the American people as a whole is that the Russians are responsible for the relentlessly escalating arms race. You cannot trust them, say Americans. They keep creating and building more and more weapons in an effort to get the upper hand on us, and so, in order to prevent them from doing so, we have to build more weapons to maintain parity. It's not America but Russia that is responsible for the arms race. We are an innocent, peace-loving nation, while the Russians are relentlessly war-like.

History Shows U.S. Militarism

This ignores the facts of history. Indeed, it is so at variance with the facts that it would be ludicrous if it were not such a grave threat to the survival of civilized life. Look back at a few of the facts in the thirty-five-year history of the arms race. Which country invented the atomic bomb? The U.S. did. And it was four years before Russia could catch up with us. Which country, then, went on to first develop the infinitely more powerful hydrogen bomb? The U.S. Which country first built and deployed intercontinental ballistic missiles tipped with nuclear warheads? The U.S. Who was first in developing nuclear submarines able to fire nuclear missiles more than a thousand miles, in developing missiles with multiple warheads, cruise missiles, mini-nukes, neutron bombs, and the massive MX missile system? The U.S. was first in all of these achievements. In the thirty-five years since WW II, every step forward in the arms race has been initiated by our country. Nor is this all. . . .

The fact is the Russians have to struggle and sweat to keep up with us in the arms race. We are far more productive than they are, and we produce weapons of far greater technological complexity and effectiveness. Their tanks are crude compared to ours. Their planes cannot match ours. We are simply far more developed technologically than they are, have much greater wealth.

It is a well-known fact that the U.S. has far more nuclear

warheads than the Russians, and when you consider the factors of accuracy and killing power, we are even further ahead. Actually, the quantity is no longer a critical factor since the U.S. and Russia between them have more than enough nuclear bombs to obliterate each other several times. And they continue to produce more each day at enormous expense!

Our country is vulnerable to nuclear attack only from Russia; Russia, on the other hand, could easily be hit with nuclear missiles fired from Britain, France, China, or the U.S. The U.S.S.R. is, of course, also vulnerable to ground attack from powerful NATO forces on the west and from a very large Chinese army in the east.

Russian Threat Is Fantasy

We Americans see the Russians as a monstrous military threat. This is largely fantasy. The Russians see themselves as surrounded, hemmed in, overpowered by the military forces of their enemies. They are scared. Their country has been invaded many times, most recently in the 1940's by Germany; and twenty million Russians died in that invasion. That kind of historical event leaves a deep scar.

That vigorous anti-communist Secretary of State, John Foster Dulles, said in 1949 that the Soviet government "does not contemplate the use of war as an instrument of its national policy." This was true then, and it's still true. They know they can't win a war with us. They don't want to suffer the kind of staggering casualties they sustained during World War II.

They know they can't defeat us in a war. But their philosophy teaches them that, one by one, the capitalist nations will collapse, that socialism, then communism, will emerge. All they have to do is encourage this inevitable historical development. All they have to do is support revolutions, wherever they crop up.

We have by far the upper hand in the arms race; but the Russians are doing very well with this other kind of aggression. We have to become conscious of the reality of our situation, and stop governing ourselves by fears, fantasies, and distortions of the facts. We need to look squarely at the meaning of nuclear war, face the fact that it means extinction.

Since we have led the way in the arms race, it is quite likely that, if we take the initiative, we can lead the way toward disarmament and world cooperation.

"It is not the nature of the military man that accounts for war, but the nature of man . . . . Aggression is part of us, as innate as eating."

Human Nature Is Responsible

Barbara W. Tuchman

Barbara W. Tuchman, the noted historian, was awarded a Pulitzer prize for two of her books, *The Guns of August* and *Stillwell and the American Experience in China.* In the following viewpoint, she claims that it is the nature of every human to fight for food or territory or dominance. She believes that the Vietnam War was not caused by the aggressive nature of America's military, but instead by the aggressive nature of America's voters who allowed Congress to fund the war.

As you read, consider the following questions:

1. Why does the author claim the military is now used more for political and ideological ends than it has been in the past?
2. Why does the author state that if blame is to be assessed for the Vietnam War it should not be placed on the military?
2. What explanation does the author give for human aggression and the military's responsibility for it?
4. Why does the author claim the draft is important?

Reprinted by permission of Russell & Volkening, Inc., as agents for the author. Copyright © 1972 by Barbara Tuchman.

The relation of the civilian citizen to the military is a subject usually productive of instant emotion and very little rational thinking.

Peace-minded people seem to disapprove study of the soldier on the theory that if starved of attention he will eventually vanish. That is unlikely. Militarism is simply the organized form of natural aggression. The same people who march to protest in the afternoon will stand in line that evening to see the latest in sadistic movies and thoroughly enjoy themselves watching blood and pain, murder, torture and rape.

To register one's dissent from the war in Vietnam by expressing disgust for the military and turning one's back on whatever shape the military wears is a natural impulse. But the error of that war, together with two other developments – the newly acquired permanence of the military role in our society and the shift to an all-volunteer force – are powerful, urgent reasons why more enlightened and better-educated citizens should *not* turn their backs and not abdicate their responsibility for controlling military policies.

Earlier in this century the French writer Julien Benda elaborated his thesis of "the treason of the intellectuals." He accused them of betraying the life of the mind and the realm of reason by descending into the arena of political, social and national passions. Now we have a treason of the intellectuals in reverse. While military-industrial and military-political interests penetrate all policy-making and add their weight to every political decision, the enlightened citizen refuses his participation, climbs out of the arena and leaves control to the professionals of war.

A Change of Military Roles

Let us look at the facts of the case.

A fundamental change in the role of the American military has taken place . . . since the advent of the atomic bomb. Paradoxically, total war has been backed off the stage by the total weapon with its uncritical capacity for overkill. Because there is enough of it around to be mutually devastating to both sides in any conflict, nuclear firepower has become the weapon that cannot be used. Contrary to the general impression, it has reduced, not enlarged, the scope of war, with the secondary and rather sinister result that while unlimited war is out, limited war is in, not as a last resort in the old-fashioned way, but as the regular, on-going support of policy.

War used to be the extension of policy by military means.

Since no political objective can now be secured with benefit by opening a nuclear war, we have narrowed ourselves to wars on the "advisory" or "assistance" level so as to mold the affairs of the client country to suit the adviser's purpose.

This development means that the military arm will be used more for political and ideological ends than in the past and that because of chronic commitment and the self-multiplying business of deterrence and a global strategy of preparedness for two-and-a-half wars – or whatever is this week's figure – the technological, industrial and governmental foundations for this enterprise have become so gigantic, extended and pervasive that they affect every act of government and consequently all our lives. . . .

There are defense plants or installations in 363 out of the 435 congressional districts in this country – in five-sixths of the total.

Who benefits? Who profits? Who lobbies in Congress to keep them in operation or to attract new plants where there are none? If you say it is the Pentagon, do not forget the local merchants and manufacturers, the local labor unions and employers and the local congressman whom we put there and whom we can recall. Who pays for our present military budget? The taxpayers – who also have the vote.

Civilian Control and Responsibility

Traditionally, the American Army has considered itself the neutral instrument of state policy. It exists to carry out the government's orders and when ordered into action does not ask "Why?" or "What for?" But the more it is used for political ends and the more deeply its influence pervades government, the less it can retain the stance of innocent instrument. The same holds true of the citizen. Our innocence too is flawed.

The fundamental American premise has always been civilian control of the military. The Vietnam War is a product of civilian policy shaped by three successive civilian presidents and their academic and other civilian advisers. The failure to end the war is also in the last resort civilian, since it is a failure by Congress to cut off appropriations.

And where does that failure trace back to? To where the vote is. I feel bewildered when I hear that easy empty slogan, "Power to the People!" Is there any country in the world whose people has more?

To blame the military for this shameful war and renounce with disgust any share in their profession is a form of escapism. It

allows the anti-war civilian to feel virtuous and uninvolved in the shame. It allows someone else to do the soldier's job which is essential to an organized state and which in the long run protects the security of the high-minded civilian while he claims it is a job too dirty for him.

Certainly the conduct of this war, perhaps *because* it is purposeless and inane, has led to abominations and inhumanities by the military which cannot be forgiven and for which the West Pointer with his motto of Duty, Honor, Country, is as much responsible as the semi-educated Lieutenant Calleys commissioned through OCS. But as one officer said, "We have the Calleys because those Harvard bastards won't fight" – Harvard being shorthand for *all* deferred college students.

Perhaps if there had been more college bastards instead of Calleys, there might have been mutinies or sit-downs instead of My Lais – certainly a preferable alternative. . . .

Human Nature Is the Culprit

The liberal's sneer at the military man does himself no honor, nor does it mark him as the better man. Military men are people. There are good ones and bad ones, some thoughtful and intelligent, some dim-wits and dodos, some men of courage and integrity, some slick operators and sharp practisers, some scholars and fighters, some braggarts and synthetic heroes. The profession contains perhaps an over-supply of routinized thinking, servility to rank and right-wing super patriots, but every group has undesirable qualities that are occupationally induced.

Mind vs. Heart

To judge from the history of mankind, we shall be compelled to conclude that the fiery destructive passions of war reign in the human breast with much more powerful sway than the mild and beneficent sentiments of peace; and that to model our political systems upon speculations of lasting tranquility, is to calculate on the weaker springs of the human character.

Alexander Hamilton, *The Federalist*, 1788.

It is not the nature of the military man that accounts for war, but the nature of man. The soldier is merely one shape that nature takes. Aggression is part of us, as innate as eating or copulating. As a student of the human record, I can say with confidence that peace is *not* the norm. Historians have calculated that up until the Industrial Revolution belligerent action

occupied more man hours than any other activity except agriculture.

Human society started with the tribe – with a sense of "We" as opposed to "They." Tribe A can have no sense of identity unless it is conscious of the otherness of Tribe B. All life and thought and action, according to the anthropologist Levi-Strauss, is based on this state of binary opposites: heaven and earth, earth and water, dark and light, right and left, north and south, male and female. These poles are not necessarily hostile but hostility *is* inherrent between the poles of We and They. When the tribes become conscious of otherness, they fight – for food or territory or dominance. This is inescapable and probably eternal. Students around the country and sympathetic faculty will not make it go away by chasing ROTC off campus, no matter how understandable the motive.

Freud called it the death-wish, meaning self-destruction. It could just as well be called the life-wish because it is an active instinct, a desire to fight, to conquer and, if also to kill, then to kill not self but others. The instinct says "I shall conquer, I shall live." It is also a male instinct. Women, being child-bearers, have a primary instinct to preserve life. . . .

"Our permanent enemy," said William James in 1904, "is the rooted bellicosity of human nature. A millenium of peace would not breed the fighting instinct out of our bone and marrow." Has anything occurred in our century – the "Terrible Twentieth" Churchill called it – to suggest that James was wrong?

What this suggests is that we should face the military element rather than turn our backs on it, learn about it, even participate in it through ROTC. If the college-educated youths become the reserve officers upon whom the Army depends then they are in a position to exert influence. . . .

Civilian Participation Is Necessary

Our form of democracy – the political system which is the matrix of our liberties – rests upon the citizen's participation, not excluding – indeed especially including – participation in the armed forces. That was the great principle of the French Revolution: the nation in arms, meaning the people in arms as distinct from a professional standing army. The nation in arms was considered the safeguard of the Republic, the guarantor against tyranny and military *coups d' etat.*

The same idea underlies the fundamental American principle of the right to bear arms as guaranteed by our Bill of Rights for the specific purpose of maintaining "a well-regulated Militia" to

protect "the security of a free state." To serve the state is what the Constitution meant, not, as the Gun Lobby pretends, the right to keep a pistol under your pillow and shoot at whomever you want to. To serve under arms in this sense is not only a right but a criterion of citizenship.

To abdicate the right because our armed forces are being used in a wrong war is natural. Nobody wants to share in or get killed in an operation that is both wicked and stupid. But we must realize that this rejection abdicates a responsibility of citizenship and contributes to an already dangerous development – the reappearance of the standing army. That is what is happening as a consequence of the change-over to an all volunteer force. We will have an army even more separate, more isolated and possibly alienated from civilian society than ever. Military men have always cherished a sense of separateness from the civilian sector, a sense of special calling deriving from their choice of a profession involving the risk of life. They feel this separateness confers a distinction that compensates them to some extent for the risk of the profession, just as the glitter and pomp and brilliant uniforms and social prestige used to compensate the armies of Europe.

For the United States the draft was the great corrective – or would have been if it had worked properly. The draft has an evil name because it would have dragged young people into an evil war. Yet it remains the only way, if administered justly, to preserve the principle of the nation in arms. The college deferrals made it a mockery. The deferral system was as anti-democratic and elitist (to use the favorite word of those who consider themselves equalizers) as anything that has ever happened in the United States. I may be happy that it kept my kin and the sons of some of my friends out of Vietnam, but I am none the less ashamed of it.

We need to re-admit some common sense into conventional liberal thinking – or feeling about the military. It seems to me urgent that we understand our relationship to the soldier's task free of emotion.

I know of no problem so subject as this one to what the late historian, Richard Hofstadter, called "the imbecile catchwords of our era like 'repression' and 'imperialism' which have had all the meaning washed out of them." Those who yell these words, he wrote, "simply have no idea what they are talking about."

The role of the military in our lives has become too serious a matter to be treated to this kind of slogan-thinking, or nonthinking.

"Militarism – as I define it – is a system institutionalizing the use of technology and force to control society. It is justified by the concept that the 'human nature' (of men) is intrinsically aggressive and competitive."

Militarism and Sexism Control America

Lyla Hoffman

Lyla Hoffman is a long-term peace activist who has spent the last ten years on the staff of the Council on Interracial Books for Children. In the following viewpoint, she claims that the cause of militarism is the patriarchal system of male control over society. In her view, militarism is based on the concept of female obedience to male authority. She claims that militarism glorifies the "masculine" military heros and "loyal soldier" stereotypes, thus perpetuating a militaristic society.

As you read, consider the following questions:

1. How does the author define militarism and patriarchy? How does she relate these systems to sexism?
2. What evidence does she present to support her claim that militarism, patriarchy and sexism control American society? Do you agree?
3. What remedy does she recommend? Do you agree?

Lyla Hoffman, "Feminist Education – A Key to Peace," *Council for Interracial Books for Children Bulletin*, Vol. 13, nos. 6 and 7.

Feminism is crucial to disarmament because we must dismantle mental – as well as military – weapons. The nuclear arms race is not simply madness – it is socially imposed *manliness* taken to its extreme."

Donna Warnock, *WIN* (Workshop in Non-Violence) Magazine, April 19, 1982.

Militarism and the arms race have yet to be widely addressed as basic "women's issues," although feminists are increasingly aware that militarism is really an extreme form of sexism. It is dependent upon sexism for its existence, and it is destructive to all feminist aspirations and ideals. This article will explore militarism in that theoretical framework before addressing the role of educators (of either sex) who believe in feminist principles.

Militarism and Patriarchy

Militarism – as I define it – is a system institutionalizing the use of technology and force to control society. It is justified by the concept that the "human nature" (of men) is intrinsically aggressive and competitive. If one accepts this concept, it follows that organized military strength is required to control society, to regulate nations and to defend one's homeland. It is necessary to defend the interests of "us" – the civilized "good-guys" –against "them" – the aggressive "bad-guys." A similar concept of "human nature" – in expanded form – is also the justification for patriarchy.

Patriarchy is a worldwide system institutionalizing a hierarchy of male control over females, children and the economic, social and political order. While ultimate control rests in the hands of a small, elite group of men, patriarchy supports the power of the individual men in their private spheres of influence. Like militarism, it is based on the concept that the "human nature" of males is aggressive and competitive. Moreover, patriarchy posits that innate "masculine" gender characteristics include dominance, strength and superior intellectual abilities, while innate "feminine" gender characteristics include weakness, passivity and nurturance. Thus militarism and patriarchy both perceive biology as destiny. Both are based on the glorification of so-called "masculine" traits and on contempt for so-called "feminine" traits. Both *require* sexist socialization of each generation to justify and maintain their existence. "Masculine" males are needed to compete, fight and rule. "Feminine" females are needed to support and cheer their males and to nurture the next generation of soldiers, workers and cheerleaders.

Think about the socialization of young boys. Training to be

79

tough, strong and competitive – not a crybaby or a sissy, not like a girl – is part of it. Striving to be *the* strongest, *the* winner – whatever the cost – is another part. Male-dominated sports, businesses, politics and wars are conducted by these "masculine" principles. Education prepares males to participate in all those games, and prepares females to cheer them on. Males who *don't* play by the "masculine" rules are belittled as cowards or "losers." They might just as well have been born female and are often mocked in that manner. The male role models on TV, in comics, in movies, in history books are all powerful – cops, superthings, generals – ever ready to kill, maim or destroy for a righteous

© 1982 The Washington Post Company. Reprinted with permission.

cause. Next best to being The Number One Hero is to be his loyal follower. The winner and his cronies always deserve the spoils – respect, power, beautiful and admiring women, the turf or country in question. The messages we give our children are that righteousness, strength and victory go hand in hand (and the rare exceptions merely prove the rule).

If socialization of *both* sexes stressed cooperation, kindness, nurturance, respect for human feelings and for human differences, patriarchy – as well as militarism – would be doomed. Neither could exist without sexist ideology. Patriarchy could not exist without the threat of force and violence to keep rebellious women and non-elite men in their place. Wars would not be fought by people who believed in the non-violent resolution of conflicts.

Militarism and Sexism

Patriarchy, militarism and sexism are all interwoven. Young people need to understand that social justice/equality issues and peace issues are related, and their links need to be underscored to make the most effective education possible.

More complex corollaries between these two "isms" were pointed out by Betty Reardon in a pioneering article titled, "Militarism and Sexism, Influences on Education for War" (*United Ministries for Education Connexion,* Fall, 1981). Reardon stresses that, "All education and socialization are conditioned by social values, and a strong case can be made that contemporary social values produce a predisposition to war." Those social values, she argues, are militarism and sexism. She points out that both are based on the concept of human nature as a "fixed order" and depend on maintaining conformity to that "fixed order." Reardon also offers some interesting comparisons between women and soldiers, that is, the ordinary G.I. who follows orders and leaders, not generals or commanders. She states:

> The most admirable virtues of the unknown soldier to whose heroism so many nations have dedicated elaborate monuments – anonymous service and sacrifice for the sake of others – are as well the virtues of the archetypal wife and mother. What the soldier has done for the nation or the warrior for the tribe through centuries of doing what was expected of him, woman has done for the family. She has been, since time immemorial, trained to sublimate her own needs to the service of others. Soldiers and mothers have days on which society offers thanks for their sacrifices by reminding them that for such they were born and by such they will continue to be identified and find meaning; for war and domesticity are in the natural order of things, as are the fixed roles of soldiers and mothers within that order. . . .

While we promote children's analytic capacities to question

The Military-Industrial Complex

Our military organization today bears little relation to that known by any of my predecessors in peacetime, or indeed by the fighting men of World War II or Korea.

Until the latest of our world conflicts, the United States had no armaments industry. American makers of plowshares could, with time and as required, make swords as well. But now we can no longer risk emergency improvisation of national defense; we have been compelled to create a permanent armaments industry of vast proportions. Added to this, three and a half million men and women are directly engaged in the defense establishment. We annually spend on military security more than the net income of all United States corporations.

This conjunction of an immense military establishment and a large arms industry is new in the American experience. The total influence – economic, political, even spiritual – is felt in every city, every State house, every office of the Federal government. We recognize the imperative need for this development. Yet we must not fail to comprehend its grave implications. Our toil, resources and livelihood are all involved; so is the very structure of our society.

In the councils of government, we must guard against the acquisition of unwarranted influence, whether sought or unsought, by the military-industrial complex. The potential for the disastrous rise of misplaced power exists and will persist.

We must never let the weight of this combination endanger our liberties or democratic processes. We should take nothing for granted. Only an alert and knowledgeable citizenry can compel the proper meshing of the huge industrial and military machinery of defense with our peaceful methods and goals, so that security and liberty may prosper together.

Taken from President Dwight D. Eisenhower's farewell radio and television address to the American people on January 17, 1961.

---

female obedience to male authority, let us also question the "masculine" military hero or "loyal soldier" stereotypes. Further, if Reardon's thesis is valid, let us as feminist educators act as peace educators – actively opposing militaristic values and ventures. To not consider militarism as a "woman's issue" weakens the struggle against patriarchal values. Militaristic rulers cannot afford challenges to behaviors and values based on gender roles. Their credibility is at stake, as is their ability to control. As feminists challenge militaristic/patriarchal values and beliefs, they can help lead to the end of militarism.

Some feminists do not oppose militarism because they fear they would reinforce the stereotype of women as "earth mother" and nurturer – a "natural" protector of life – and thus weaken

feminist arguments against biology as destiny. But feminists have always argued that socialization, not biology, is destiny; females are *trained* to nurture. Why shouldn't feminists promote the training of *all* human beings to be nurturing "earth parents" – with *everyone* protecting human life and our environment? Feminists strive to convince men to share nurturing roles in the home and family; why not strive for men and women to nurture life in the world at large?

Today humankind is witnessing the ultimate power play of militaristic, patriarchal rulers. These rulers have usurped the power of Nature (or God or Goddess, as you believe) to decide if, and how, life on Earth will continue. How can feminists stand aside without taking action? How can educators ignore this threat to existence? . . .

Militarism has also been defined as a "male-bonding institution of specialists in violence." Violence – or the threat of violence – is directly or indirectly used to control women, people of color, poor people and other nations. Many feminists believe that violence is *never* justified, not even in the service of a revolution for liberation from oppression. Many call for inventive alternatives to violence and war. Other feminists in the peace movement deplore all violence but believe that oppressed people must themselves decide upon the methods for achieving their freedom. (Violence may not be the method of *choice* in such cases, but it may be the means of last resort, particularly in the face of the organized violence of a despotic state.) Whatever our opinions on revolutionary violence or on total non-violence, we can address militarism as part of patriarchal institutions.

Militarism vs. Feminism

Militarism directly contradicts a number of feminist goals:

1. *Feminists are concerned about nurturing and caring.* Soldiers are trained to kill without caring. The feminist educator's goal is to develop nurturing skills in both sexes, as well as the skill to develop warm, open, equal relationships between people. Military training does the opposite.

2. *Feminists are concerned about "choice"* – the right to choose if, how and when to bear a child; the right to choose any vocation or life style; the right to choose the type of medical care one considers best; the right to choose life over death. What mockery *any* war, let alone nuclear war, makes of these choices. Even the use of "peaceful" nuclear power, decided upon by a small group of men, poses special radiation danger to women and children of this and future generations. The feminist educator's

goal is to encourage young people to recognize and choose among many life options. War rules out such choices. Even government budgets reflecting an arms race rules out many life options.

3. *Feminists are concerned about shared decision-making.* Decisions about developing, stockpiling and deploying arms – and about foreign policy – are made by males in Congress and the Pentagon (or their counterparts in other nations). The occasional appearance of a Margaret Thatcher – or some other female who plays by "masculine" values and rules and is totally surrounded by male advisors – does not alter the fact that military decisions are made by male "experts." And feminists have ample reason to distrust so-called "experts" in all fields, who use technology and expertise to mystify and monopolize authority. (And who have consistently lied to us on nuclear issues.)

Feminist educators strive to teach by using non-authoritarian processes and to build upon respect for each student's experience and differences while developing their abilities for responsible decision-making. Militarism, which teaches unquestioning obedience, has contrary processes and goals.

4. *Feminists are concerned about violence, particularly against women and children.* Nothing does greater violence than war – except nuclear war. Feminist educators strive to assist children's developmental and physical health and to teach non-violence.

5. *Feminists are concerned about women and children living in poverty.* Money is being withheld from programs for the poor and used to increase the military budget. Consider the effect of such decisions on the 81 per cent of welfare families with children that are headed by women (a disproportionate share of them women of color). Consider the effects on the nation's poor – 70 per cent of whom are women, with a high percentage of them women of color, older women, disabled women. Internationally, money spent by Third World countries on military arms is one reason money is not directed to alleviate women and children's illiteracy, hunger and poor health. Such spending is contrary to feminist educators' goal of equal educational and life opportunities for all girls and women.

6. *Feminists are concerned with sex-role socialization.* They do not want either sex to become violent, aggressive or dominant. Militarism demands those qualities (in males).

84

What Feminist Educators Can Do

Feminist educators have heretofore concentrated on changing the sex-role socialization of girls. They now might consider shifting their present emphasis from what girls and women – as well as boys and men – can do to what boys and men – as well as girls and women – must do. And what boys and men must do is to learn nurturance and non-violence. Can't *all* young people be helped to understand that the traditional way that boys reach manhood contributes to the appeal of militarism – and towards militarism's ultimate battle, nuclear war?

Just as feminist educators have devised imaginative ways to challenge sexism in language arts, history, math, music – all school curriculums – so can they devise effective ways of challenging militarism in curriculums. We can become more assertive in promoting "feminine" values. Peaceful conflict resolution and peace education can be developed and introduced at all grade levels. New courses can be designed and popularized. Parental support, as well as administrative support, can be mobilized. New concepts of patriotism, of security, of nationalism, of heroism can be developed. An understanding of global interdependence is also required. Visions of a peaceful world need to be developed so that children (and we adults) do not despair.

Militarism in a nuclear world *can* be confronted. Educators have a special responsibility to do so, thus ensuring the survival of future generations.

> *"The basic rule of Soviet behavior was laid down years ago by Lenin: Probe with bayonets. If you encounter steel, withdraw. If you encounter mush, continue."*

America Is at War

Richard Nixon

Richard Nixon was President of the United States from 1969 until his resignation in August 1974. Since leaving office, he has published several books including *Memoirs* (1978), *The Real War* (1980) and *Leaders* (1982). In the following viewpoint taken from *The Real War*, he claims that America is rapidly drifting into an international political situation where it will be confronted with a choice between surrender and suicide.

As you read, consider the following questions:

1. Why does President Nixon claim the "struggle with the Soviets will continue to dominate world events for the rest of this century"?
2. What is the *legacy of the 1960s* that concerns President Nixon?
3. What are the President's thoughts on U.S. disarmament?
4. President Nixon claims the Soviets are ruled by the sword and America by the spirit. Would the author of the preceding viewpoint agree? Do you?

The Soviet Union today is the most powerfully armed expansionist nation the world has ever known, and its arms buildup continues at a pace nearly twice that of the United States. There is no mystery about Soviet intentions. The Kremlin leaders do not want war, but they do want the world. And they are rapidly moving into position to get what they want.

In the 1980s America for the first time in modern history will confront two cold realities. The first of these is that if war were to come, we might lose. The second is that we might be defeated without war. The second prospect is more likely than the first, and almost as grim. The danger facing the West during the balance of this century is less that of a nuclear holocaust than it is of drifting into a situation in which we find ourselves confronted with a choice between surrender and suicide – red or dead. That danger can still be averted, but the time in which we can avert it is rapidly running out.

The Crisis We Face

The next two decades represent a time of maximum crisis for America and for the West, during which the fate of the world for generations to come may well be determined.

Other nations have much longer experience than we have in the use of power to maintain the peace. But they no longer have the power. So, by default, the world looks to the United States. It looks today with nervous apprehension, as the bulwarks against Soviet expansion crumble in one nation after another, and as the United States appears so lost in uncertainty or paralyzed by propriety that it is either unable or unwilling to act.

Soviet ambitions present the United States with a strategic challenge of global proportion, which requires a renewed strategic consciousness and response. It requires a coherent national strategy based upon informed public support. Piecemeal temporizing will not do. Angola, Ethiopia, Afghanistan, South Yemen, Mozambique, Laos, Cambodia, and South Vietnam, all have been brought under communist domination since 1974; nearly 100 million people in the last five years. Iran has been plunged into bloody chaos and turned overnight from a bastion of Western strength to a cauldron of virulent anti-Westernism, its oil treasures lying provocatively exposed to lustful Russian eyes. Cuba acts increasingly as an agent of wide-ranging Soviet ambitions. These are examples of how the pieces will continue to fall if we take a piecemeal approach. We have to recover the geopolitical momentum, marshaling and using our resources in

the tradition of a great power.

The old colonial empires are gone. The new Soviet imperialism requires a new counterforce to keep it in check. The United States cannot provide this alone, but without strong and effective leadership from the United States, it cannot be provided at all. We cannot afford to waffle and waver. Either we act like a great power or we will be reduced to a minor power, and thus reduced we will not survive – nor will freedom or Western values survive. . . . We are at war. We are engaged in a titanic struggle in which the fates of nations are being decided. . . .

The Legacy of the 1960s

The basic rule of Soviet behavior was laid down years ago by Lenin: Probe with bayonets. If you encounter steel, withdraw. If you encounter mush, continue. The question is which will the Soviets encounter: steel or mush? . . .

Unfortunately, America is still suffering from the legacy of the 1960s. A rabid anti-intellectualism swept the nation's campuses then, and fantasy reigned supreme. Attacks on anything representing the established order were in fashion. The discords of that decade and of its aftermath critically weakened the nation's capacity to meet its responsibilities in the world, not only militarily but also in terms of its ability to lead.

Ironically, even as anti-intellectualism ravaged the campuses, the 1960s also saw an overly "intellectualized" new fashion take hold among many of those who thought professionally about arms and particularly about arms control: the notion that above a certain minimum, the less military strength you had, the better. The hope arose that if the United States limited its own arms, others – particularly the Soviets – would follow. But the Soviets did not perform according to theory. In fact, during the same period when this arms-control doctrine was winning favor among American theorists, and the theorists were winning influence, the Soviet five-year plans were charting ever greater increases in military spending, clearly guided by coherent strategic objectives. The Soviets were not bogged down in theory; they were driving toward supremacy.

There are many today who suggest that American civilization is suffering a terminal illness, that we are witnessing the beginning of the end of the West. Some American opinion leaders view this with despair. Some, especially in darkest academia, see it as the logical and overdue result of our being on the wrong side. Like the classic definition of fox hunting as "the unspeakable in pursuit of the uneatable," they see America as the

aggressive in support of the oppressive. As playwright Eugene Ionesco reported after a recent visit to the United States, American intellectuals tend to be "masochists who want to be blamed for everything wrong in the world." When he told American liberal friends that the United States was not as bad as other nations, "the liberals looked at me askance. For in order to be appreciated in America, one must, above all, never say that Americans are not the worst criminals of humanity." . . .

We Have No Time To Lose

Woodrow Wilson once eloquently declared World War I a war to make the world "safe for democracy." However noble that intent, events soon made a mockery of it. Our aim must be a world within which democracy will be safe, but more fundamentally a world in which aggression is restrained and national independence secure. Just as the 1940s and 1950s saw the end of the old colonialism, the 1980s and 1990s must be the years in which we turn back the new Soviet imperialism. To chart our course for the future, we must know our enemies, understand our friends, and know ourselves – where we are, how we got here, and where we want to go.

To meet the challenge to our own survival and to the survival of freedom and peace, we must drastically increase our military power, shore up our economic power, reinvigorate our willpower, strengthen the power of our Presidents, and develop a strategy aimed not just at avoiding defeat but at attaining victory. . . .

It was shortly before the outbreak of World War II that General Douglas MacArthur observed, "The history of failure in war can be summed up in two words: Too Late." MacArthur, then in the Philippines, had seen the war clouds on the horizon; he had been frustrated in his efforts to win support for a strengthening of forces in the Philippines. He warned of the danger, but too many said, "So what?"

When he made that statement the atomic bomb had not yet burst on Hiroshima, forever changing the potential nature of war and the consequences of a surprise attack. The United States had time to recover from a naval Pearl Harbor, and it had ample warning of impending war. We could have less than thirty minutes' warning of a nuclear Pearl Harbor, from which we would have no time to recover. The time to prevent that from happening is now. There is no time to lose. . . .

Disarmament Threatens U.S. Survival

In considering the military balance between East and West it is important to remember that the two sides arm for different

Ten Rules

If I could carve ten rules into the walls of the Oval Office for my successors to follow in the dangerous years just ahead, they would be these:

1. Always be prepared to negotiate, but never negotiate without being prepared.
2. Never be belligerent, but always be firm.
3. Always remember that covenants should be openly agreed to but privately negotiated.
4. Never seek publicity that would destroy the ability to get results.
5. Never give up unilaterally what could be used as a bargaining chip. Make your adversaries give something for everything they get.
6. Never let your adversary underestimate what you *would* do in response to a challenge. Never tell him in advance what you would *not* do.
7. Always leave your adversary a face-saving line of retreat.
8. Always carefully distinguish between friends who provide some human rights and enemies who deny all human rights.
9. Always do at least as much for our friends as our adversaries do for our enemies.
10. Never lose faith. In a just cause faith can move mountains. Faith without strength is futile, but strength without faith is sterile.

Having laid down these rules, I would also suggest that the President keep in his desk drawer, in mind but out of sight, an eleventh commandment: When saying "always" and "never," always keep a mental reservation; never foreclose the unique exception; always leave room for maneuver. "Always" and "never" are guideposts, but in high-stakes diplomacy there are few immutables. A President always has to be prepared for what he thought he would never do.

Richard M. Nixon

purposes. The Soviets have been engaged in a determined arms race because they want strategic superiority over the United States, and every year their effort has continued to increase. Our effort has not kept pace. It has, in fact, declined. In the 1960s the United States deliberately adopted the McNamara doctrine of self-restraint, which was intended to induce a reciprocal Soviet restraint and lead to arms limitation agreements that would benefit both sides. Instead, the Soviets have taken advantage of it to further their own drive for superiority. The Soviets have raced, and the United States has not; the result has been a rapid change in strategic balance virtually unprecedented in history. Not only have the efforts of the two sides differed, but so have their views of the nature of the competition. In the West arms

are maintained as a necessity of defense; in the East arms are maintained to achieve the expansion of Soviet power. So the "arms race" is not a race between two contenders with the same goal. It is now more nearly akin to the race between hunter and hunted. If the hunted wins, both live; if the hunter wins, only one lives.

This imbalance of intentions affects the balance of power. It gives the Soviets the aggressor's edge. The aggressor chooses the time and place of combat, whether in the jungles of Vietnam, a strike into central Europe, or an intercontinental nuclear exchange. We have to offset this aggressor's edge by effective deterrence, whether by the superiority of our forces or by the skill and determination with which we use them. To create an equilibrium in the conflict – to preserve our safety – we need either more power to offset their inherent advantage or clear evidence that our will to use our power to defend our interests is equal to theirs. This is the context in which we should consider the strategic balance. . . .

The Sword and the Spirit

The U.S.-Soviet contest is a struggle between two opposite poles of human experience – between those represented by the sword and by the spirit, by fear and by hope. Their system is ruled by the sword; ours is governed by the spirit. Their influence has spread by conquest; ours has spread by example. This struggle is not new. It did not begin with the end of World War II, or with the Russian Revolution. It is as old as civilization. And history gives no sure guide to the outcome, for it shows us that through the centuries first one side has prevailed, and then the other. The struggle is as old as the drive of rulers to impose tyranny and of people to escape it; as old as the effort of one nation to conquer and of others to resist. Tyrannies have risen and fallen; so have democracies. Man has struggled against oppression and won; oppressors also have won. . . .

In America, the spirit is there, if only the spark can be found to light it. As Churchill once said, "We have not journeyed all this way across the centuries, across the oceans, across the mountains, across the prairies, because we are made of sugar candy."

America's greatest strength in this global contest is America itself – our people, our land, our system, our culture, our tradition, our reputation. American history is full of archetypal heroes: the stony Vermont farmer, the Pennsylvania coal miner, the Southern gentleman farmer, the Texas oilman, the Las Vegas

gambler, the California gold miner, the Oregon lumberjack – the list is extensive. Cowboys, robber barons, pioneers, traders, roughnecks, and horse thieves – all share a common trait that is cherished in American folklore: individuality. We have always prized and encouraged the individual. The acceptance of individual differences has been our hallmark.

Americans also are a generous people. We have shown ourselves willing to help others anywhere on the globe. We have extended aid and encouraged development in the rest of the world, because we have been conditioned by our history to see good in growth. We want independent, self-reliant neighbors and prosperous trading partners, nations joined with us in the sort of common interest that benefits us all. This is why the United States has friends and allies, while the Soviet Union has subjects and satellites.

From George Washington's Neutrality Proclamation through the Monroe Doctrine and the Marshall Plan runs an American impulse that disdains war and instead seeks to spread freedom and prosperity. We have a natural respect for the individuality of others, and a concern for their well-being. These instincts make for a constructive foreign policy, one that commands the genuine respect of other nations – *if* we also show the resolve required of a great power. . . .

Our Cause Is Right

Victory without war requires that we resolve to use our strength in ways short of war. There is today a vast gray area between peace and war, and the struggle will be largely decided in that area. If we expect to win without war, or even not to lose without war, then we must engage the adversary within that area. We need not duplicate his methods, but we must counter them – even if that means behaving in ways other than we would choose to in an ideal world.

The uses of power cannot be divorced from the purposes of power. The old argument over whether "the end justifies the means" is meaningless in the abstract; it has meaning only in concrete terms of whether a particular end justifies a particular means. The true test of idealism comes in its results. Some ends of transcendent moral value do justify some means that would not be justified in other circumstances.

Preserving liberty is a moral goal, defeating aggression is a moral goal, avoiding war is a moral goal, establishing conditions that can maintain peace with freedom through our children's generation is a moral goal. Failure to take whatever means are

needed to keep liberty alive would be an act of moral abdication.

Victory does not mean being "the world's policeman." It does mean establishing, very explicitly, that we regard the frontiers of Soviet advance as the frontiers of our own defense, and that we will respond accordingly. And it does require a firm, unflagging faith, as Lincoln would put it, that we are on God's side, that our cause is right, that we act for all mankind.

It may seem melodramatic to treat the twin poles of human experience represented by the United States and the Soviet Union as the equivalent of Good and Evil, Light and Darkness, God and the Devil; yet if we allow ourselves to think of them that way, even hypothetically, it can help clarify our perspective on the world struggle. . . .

The United States represents hope, freedom, security, and peace. The Soviet Union stands for fear, tyranny, aggression, and war. If these are not poles of good and evil in human affairs, then the concepts of good and evil have no meaning. Those who cannot see the distinction have little claim to lecture us on conscience. It is precisely because so many have "transposed the points" that the light of reason has dimmed and a dangerous confusion has spread. Ending that confusion is the first step toward seeing the path to victory.

"I'd rather be slaughtered than slaughter... that is our moral obligation."

Disarmament Is a Moral Obligation

John F. Alexander

John Alexander is coeditor of *The Other Side*, a Christian monthly magazine which describes its purpose as "justice rooted in discipleship." In the following viewpoint, Mr. Alexander argues that American possession of nuclear weapons is both impractical and immoral. He claims that the best way to combat Marxism is with ideology rather than bombs. Real power, in the author's opinion, comes from the concept of justice rooted in America's Judeo-Christian heritage and not from military might.

As you read, consider the following questions:

1. What does the author think would happen if the U.S. were to unilaterally give up its nuclear weapons?
2. Why does Mr. Alexander think that Soviet occupation of the U.S. is impossible?
3. Do you agree or disagree with the author's final statement that it is better to be killed than kill? Why?

John F. Alexander, "Bleeding Hearts: But the Russians Are Coming," *The Other Side*, October 1983. Reprinted with permission from *The Other Side*, 300 W. Apsley, Philadelphia, PA 19144.

The United States can't get rid of the bomb. If we did, the Soviet Union would soon dominate the whole world, including the United States. Unilateral nuclear disarmament is therefore impractical, irresponsible, and immoral.

In other words, the Russians are coming.

Or so I'm told.

Disarmament Makes Nuclear War Unlikely

However, unilateral disarmament has one enormous advantage. It makes all-out nuclear war extremely unlikely.

At least for now, only the United States and the Soviet Union are capable of fighting an all-out nuclear war. And if the United States gets rid of the bomb, the Soviet leaders would have no reason to use theirs on a massive scale. For example, they'd have no need to launch a first strike to destroy our missiles (which would be nonexistent). Nor would they accidentally launch an attack through misreading their radar and mistaking a flock of sea gulls for U.S. missiles.

So unilateral nuclear disarmament would virtually rule out the nightmare of nuclear annihilation we all half expect.

And there's a lot to be said for that – an awful lot.

Maybe anything *but* unilateral disarmament is impractical, irresponsible, and immoral.

However, our disarming has one big disadvantage. It gives the Soviet Union almost all the trumps. In other words, the Russians are coming.

If the United States gets rid of the bomb, what's to keep the Soviet Union from occupying the whole world? Certainly they now occupy Eastern Europe and Afghanistan, and they have vile prison camps stretching halfway around the world. I at least have no desire to spend any time in those camps.

Personally, I think that Afghanistan and Poland are enough to keep the Soviets busy for a couple of years. I doubt they are going to be in a hurry to occupy any more countries. But I could be wrong.

And in any case, even if the Soviets didn't occupy any more countries, they could use the threat of the bomb to extort almost anything they wanted from anybody they wanted. You don't have to believe in the moral perfection of the United States to think that it would be dreadful to concentrate power in the hands of the Soviet Union (or anyone else). When a bully is loose in the school yard, something can be said for a second bully to limit his depredations.

Maybe unilateral disarmament would be impractical, irrespon-

sible, and immoral.

The Bomb Is Impractical and Immoral

In other words, life is complicated. Do you want a bully loose in the school yard with no one to challenge him, or do you want two bullies who might blow up the whole school yard? That is, would you rather be red or dead?

For many years, our government has assured us that this is a false choice. They tell us that the threat of nuclear war will keep us from Soviet domination and that no nuclear exchange will ever occur. (At least, they *used* to assure us no exchange would occur.) And we must admit that to date no exchange has occurred. They have been right so far. We should give them that much.

However, the average American expects nuclear war in this generation. I do too. I think our government is wrong. Our present course will lead to nuclear annihilation. And that is simply and utterly unacceptable.

Given those choices, I'd rather be red.

But that makes it sound like a selfish concern, like I'm afraid to die. And no doubt that's part of the truth. I'm in no hurry to have the bomb dropped on me and my city.

But that's not the main point. I hope I'm willing to die to keep the Soviet Union (or anyone else) from dominating the world. But I'm not willing to annihilate the world to keep the Soviets from dominating it. Better dominated than annihilated.

But maybe I'm overstating the case. Perhaps an all-out nuclear war wouldn't annihilate the world. Perhaps some would be left alive. But if so, it would be a vile existence of genetic deformities, death by starvation and cancer – all subject to anarchic, marauding bands. I'd much prefer domination (or even annihilation).

All I'm saying is that as long as life is possible on this earth, even if dominated by the Soviet Union, we can resist totalitarianism and injustice.

Yet the button could still be pushed, and all would be lost. Domination does not eliminate the possibility of later annihilation.

So I'm convinced that keeping the bomb is impractical, irresponsible, and immoral.

Soviet Occupation Is Impossible

And my reasons go deeper. For one thing, I think military planners lack imagination. Surely everything from the Revolu-

tionary War to Vietnam to Iran to Nicaragua to El Salvador to Northern Ireland shows that superpowers can be kept from dominating – and you don't need a nuclear bomb to do it. A determined David regularly slays Goliath. We can stop the Soviets without threatening nuclear annihilation, and only a strange fixation on military might conceals that from us.

Maybe the United States lacked the "will" in Vietnam or Nicaragua, as some military planners tell us. But what about Afghanistan? If a handful of guerrillas with little more than slingshots can stop the Soviets, couldn't we? And why did the Soviet Union never seriously invade badly armed China, even when China had no bomb? Occupying a country that intends to rule itself is harder than the Pentagon ever told us. If the Pentagon limited its planning to systems of defense instead of dreaming up ever more destructive weapons of aggression, we would not need the bomb.

Superiority and Idolatry

National security policy appears to be based increasingly on the assumption that our national well-being and security are promoted primarily through the further expansion of military force, with special attention given to our nuclear capability. Military policies based on that assumption, however, when not balanced by broader understandings of security, of human needs, of the real roots of national strength and a healthy social fabric, may well undermine the very well-being and security they were designed to promote. An adequate military defense capability is one thing. The diversion of unprecedented and increasingly higher amounts of money and resources into a search for an endlessly elusive "superiority" is quite another. Such action is both self-defeating and idolatrous. It is important that every Christian, indeed every citizen, seek to understand the impact made on the general welfare of this nation by a national security policy dominated by the search for military superiority and driven by a technological imperative that is in danger of assuming a life of its own, a life which would be untrammeled by either considerations of real defense needs or moral constraints.

Taken from *To Make Peace*, a report of The Joint Commission On Peace of the Episcopal Church, published in 1982 by Forward Movement Publications.

And I for one believe those systems could be nonviolent. Look at Solidarity, with their nearly nonviolent approach. Perhaps I am too optimistic, but I still think they'll.bring the Soviets to their knees. (They've apparently had some success so far, even without detailed plans for what to do when their leaders were arrested).

What if we showed a caring spirit for the invaders? What if we

were prepared to blow up all the bridges an invading army needed? What if our technologists put their ingenuity into a new variety of weapons? What if our youth were trained in nonviolent resistance? What if ROTC focused on training underground leaders for massive civil disobedience? What if the mass of Americans believed in resistance enough to risk their lives half as much as they must daily under the nuclear umbrella? Then Soviet occupation would be out of the question.

In Denmark, when the Nazis gave the order for all Jews to wear the star of David, most complied. But so did the king and half the rest of the population. What could the Nazis do?

A Higher Power

It all boils down to a different understanding of power. Most of us believe that nuclear bombs, Polaris submarines, and ICBMs are the quintessence of power, but I suggest that having the hearts and minds of people is more powerful. All that weapons can do is kill; they cannot dominate, they cannot squash resistance, they cannot inspire. The Soviets will never rule Afghanistan until they rule the hearts of the people.

The pen is mightier than the sword, as they say. At least Marx's is. And that's the threat. The Soviets themselves have no appeal to anyone to speak of. Countries take turns breaking off diplomatic relations with them. They seem incapable of cultural penetration. So they present little threat, nuclear bomb or not.

But Marx is another matter. Oppressed people buy in because he cares, he offers answers, and he gives a name to what is devouring them. He has power because he is nearly right, because he was raised on Old Testament concepts of justice. Communism, after all, is a Judeo-Christian heresy.

If we want to combat the "red menace," bombs won't do it. Offering a better ideology than Marx might. We need to get even closer to the Bible than Marx did.

And unilateral disarmament would be an enormously powerful first step, far more powerful than any bomb. That would capture people's imaginations and hearts. (It would be a great propaganda ploy, but I really am not especially concerned about bolstering America's sagging prestige.)

I'd Rather Die Than Kill

But in all of this is one flaw. If we reject the bomb and win the minds and hearts of the world, the Soviets still might use their nuclear stranglehold. They might demand that we send everyone without calluses to Siberia. And if faced with massive resistance,

they might threaten to drop one nuclear bomb per day on urban areas until the resistance faded.

If that happened, we'd just have to quietly tell them that we couldn't do that and that they'd just have to drop their bombs on us. (And we'd have to tell France or Brazil the same thing if they threatened to use their bombs.) Odds are, they'd quickly fade themselves. But they might drop those bombs.

"... AND I SAY UNTO YOU, THOU ART BETTER DEAD THAN RED."

Reprinted with permission from *The Daily World.*

I don't think they would, but they certainly could. The Nazis didn't execute the king of Denmark, but they could have. And something nearly that ruthless happened in Chile when the communists were thrown out.

One answer is that any strategy may fail. Certainly the nuclear umbrella may, and so, I suppose, may nonviolent resistance. Nothing is foolproof.

More important is that at least then we'd be bombed rather than bombing, slaughtered rather than slaughtering. For me, the bottom line is that I'd rather be slaughtered than slaughter. The point is hard to argue, but I believe that that is our moral obligation.

Remember, Jesus, too, was slaughtered. Crucifixion is not a nice way to go. We are called to take up *our* cross, too, and should not be surprised if we wind up crucified.

The quintessence of power is not the bomb. It is the cross.

"The responsibility to defend Western civilization has fallen to the United States because of our superior wealth, resources, and technological skills."

U.S. Has Moral Duty to Defend Free World

Phyllis Schlafly

Phyllis Schlafly is the president of Eagle Forum which describes itself as a "national pro-family organization." She is the author of five books on defense and foreign policy and was a member of Ronald Reagan's 1980 Defense Advisory Group. In the following viewpoint, excerpted from a pamphlet responding to the Catholic Bishop's pastoral letter on war and peace, Ms. Schlafly states that the U.S. has become responsible for the defense of western civilization. She argues that death by nuclear war is a lesser evil than cowardice, dishonor and betrayal.

As you read, consider the following questions:

1. What role does Ms. Schlafly see the U.N. playing in working for world peace?
2. What proof does the author present to support her claim that "Not a single little country in the world needs to worry about aggression from the United States"?
3. On what basis does Ms. Schlafly claim the U.S. has a moral obligation to defend Western civilization?

Phyllis Schlafly, "The Pastoral Letter on War and Peace We Wish the Bishops Had Written." Speech presented to the Committee for Liason with Priests, Religious and Laity of the National Conference of Catholic Bishops, November 14, 1982. Saint Joan Peace Institute, A Division of Eagle Forum Education and Legal Defense Fund, 316 Pennsylvania Avenue, S.E., Suite 203, Washington, DC 20003.

It takes only one aggressive government to start a war, but it takes two to make peace. Unfortunately, the fact of a Soviet threat as well as the existence of a Soviet imperial drive for hegemony, at least in regions of major strategic interest, cannot be denied. Nor can we close our eyes to the denial of the dignity of the human person by the ruling regime in the U.S.S.R. It is the reality of our times. Those who may have forgotten the atrocities of the invasions of Poland, Lithuania, Latvia, Estonia, Hungary, and Czechoslovakia, have had abundant recent reminders in Soviet treatment of Afghanistan and Poland.

Unfortunately, an obsessive desire for detente and placebo-agreements have led some quarters to gloss over Soviet crimes against religion and humanity, and to paint the Soviet rulers as insecure, fearful men trying only to protect themselves against Western military power. but all the world knows which way the movement of peoples is stopped by barbed wire and electrified fences, mined fields, and armed guards.

We should continue to seek bilateral, verifiable agreements with the Soviet Union, but we must not succumb to the deception of nonverifiable, betrayed agreements. . . .

The missing element of world order today is the absence of a properly constituted political authority with the capacity to make or enforce the peace. Three decades ago, we hoped that the United Nations could fill that role, but the UN today is, in a popular current colloquialism, a "wimp." It is completely unable to promote peace or even to play the role of peacemaker.

Secretary-General Javier Perez de Cuellar complained to the General Assembly that the UN cannot play an effective role in settling world disputes. He candidly admitted that the UN has failed in Afghanistan, Lebanon, Iran-Iraq, the Falklands, Cyprus, Central America, Cambodia, and Poland. The UN is so dominated by the Soviet Union that the United States is routinely blamed for everything in the world while denied ordinary courtesies extended to all other member nations. We are so decisively outvoted that there is no way to assert a creative or leadership role for America in that forum.

We should not be so paralyzed in our efforts at peacemaking by sentimental attachment to a failed political dream that we ignore the central danger of the Soviet threat to the Free World. We must guard against that "softness of heart" which exposes loved ones to danger by failing to recognize the sinfulness of some powerful men. Soviet leaders have refused to recognize that their own people are human beings created in the image and likeness of God.

We readily recognize that we live in a world that is estranged from Christian values. In order to remain a Christian in the face of Soviet armed power and repeated aggression, the Free World must take a resolute stand. We must continually equip ourselves to profess the full faith of the Church, and to protect the right to practice our religion against the onslaught of a secularized, neopagan government armed with powerful weapons. . . .

Peace Through Strength

We appreciate the efforts of scientists who won the race in 1945 against the scientists of our enemies to unlock the secret of atomic power. The face of the globe would be tragically different today if the scientists working for Nazi Germany or Imperial Japan had developed the atomic weapon first. We appreciate the efforts of our scientists who have developed atomic power for peaceful purposes. (For example, nuclear power plants provide one-third of the electric power in the state of Illinois and one-half of the power in Chicago.)

Pacifism In the Face of Evil

What about the immorality of pacifism in the face of aggressive evil against those in one's custody and care?

Pacifism for the Jews meant Auschwitz. Pacifism for the Afghans means imprisonment of their country. Pacifism for Europe and the United States means the end of Western, Christian-based civilization. Pacifism for Israel today means the end of Israel. Pacifism in the face of militant Islam would have meant mosques, not churches and cathedrals, dotting Western Europe today. What kind of option is that?

Christian pacifism in the face of an aggressive communist superpower ambitious for global domination can also entail not a little moral and material freeloading at the expense of one's fellow citizens required to take the military risk and carry the moral onus of defending the right of pacifists to "speak out."

Patrick J. Buchanan. "What About Pacifism in the Face of Evil?" *The Wanderer*, November 30. 1982.

The nuclear age has been the theater of our existence for almost four decades. During that period of time, we have seen a stunning demonstration of how the nuclear weapon *in the hands of the United States* is the most powerful material vehicle for peace the world has ever known. Since 1945, we have had striking proof of the wisdom of the Gospel's formula for peace. St. Luke tells us (11:21), "When a strong man armed keepeth his palace, his goods are in peace." The Father of our Country,

George Washington, expressed the same maxim in these words: "If we desire to secure peace . . . it must be *known* that we are at all times *ready* for war." The key to security is not only military secrets, but it requires informing one's adversary publicly in advance what weapons one has and what plans exist for their use.

The United States is the "strong man" in the modern world. We proved that the surest key to peace is for America to have military superiority over all other nations in the world. That conclusion is not just speculation, not merely a hope, not an untried hypothesis, but a fact proved by historical experience of the years since 1945.

President Reagan explained this in a televised address in early 1982. During the years when the United States "could have dominated the world with no risk to itself . . . when the United States had the only undamaged industrial power in the world . . . [when] our military might was at its peak, and we alone had the ultimate weapon – the nuclear weapon – with the unquestioned ability to deliver it anywhere in the world," America chose *not* to take one single step toward aggression, imperialism, or world domination. Instead, as the President so eloquently described it, the United States followed a course "unique in all the history of mankind. We used our power and wealth to rebuild the war-ravaged economies of the world, including those of the nations who had been our enemies."

In all history, there is no record of any other government holding such power in its hands and failing to use it to assert dominion over other nations and men. We proved that the peace and freedom of the world are safe when America has nuclear superiority. Not a single little country in the world needs to worry about aggression from the United States.

During those years, Western Europe had its longest period of peace in all history because it was cradled in the safety of American nuclear superiority. The 1945 demonstration of U.S. nuclear power stopped the Russian armies from rolling any further across Europe. Winston Churchill said that there would not have been a free man left in Western Europe if it were not for the American nuclear umbrella.

In the Old Testament we read, "Beat your plowshares into swords, and your pruning hooks into spears; let the weak say, I am strong." (Joel 3:10) If what is left of the Free World is to remain free in the face of the monster weapons possessed by the Soviet Union, our first duty must be, "let the Soviets say, America is strong."

America's Responsibility

The responsibility to defend Western civilization has fallen to the United States because of our superior wealth, resources, and technological skills. The continued survival of our country, of our Church, and of our allies depends on America fulfilling its responsibilities to be the guardian of peace with freedom.

While some might wish for a simpler day in which nuclear weapons did not exist, we know it is not possible to turn back the clock. We must live with the existence of nuclear weapons on the basis of an assumption we would not tolerate in any other area of life: we know we cannot afford one mistake. Winston Churchill explained this nuclear fact of life when he said: "Sometimes in the past we have committed the folly of throwing away our arms. Under the mercy of Providence, and at great cost and sacrifice, we have been able to recreate them when the need arose. But if we abandon our nuclear deterrent, there will be no second chance. To abandon it now would be to abandon it forever."

In the parable of the talents, Jesus gave us a lesson that applies to America's nuclear responsibilities. The Lord made it clear that He rewards those who put their talents to productive and profitable use, and He punishes those who bury their talents in the ground; and, further, that He expects results in proportion to the talents He has given us. When the one man tried to excuse his failure to make profitable use of his talent by saying, "being afraid I went and hid thy talent in the earth," the Lord cast that unproductive servant into exterior darkness where there was weeping and gnashing of teeth. Fear is not an acceptable excuse. Alexander Solzhenitsyn echoed this thesis when he said, "The cost of cowardice is always evil."

Our nation has committed many sins (among them the sin of abortion), but we know that our nation bears no guilt whatsoever for threatening the peace of the world. We have proved that, no matter how many nuclear weapons America has, our might does not threaten the freedom or religion or security of any other nation, or the peace of the world.

Nevertheless, because of our preeminent position in world leadership, we cannot evade our responsibility as the principal defender of Western civilization. As the eminent Catholic theologian, Charles Cardinal Journet, stated, "If the non-Communist bloc unilaterally disarmed, it would give the world to the Soviet Empire and would betray all the holy values, temporal and spiritual, which we ought to defend: this would be the

evil of betrayal."

We must shape a climate of opinion which will make it possible for America to be militarily strong enough to fulfill these global responsibilities. By a mix of political vision and moral wisdom, we must interpret our national interest in terms of the larger global interest and assume our leadership responsibilites. Without American military strength, there is little possiblity that any nation can endure in freedom anywhere in the world.

We are fortunate that America has had political leaders who understand our nation's moral responsibilities. Former President Dwight Eisenhower, who ordered the building of the Triad of our security system (the Minuteman missiles, the Polaris/Poseidon submarines, and the B-52 bombers), said, "Until war is eliminated from international relations, unpreparedness for it is well nigh as criminal as war itself."

Nuclear war would, indeed, be horrible; but to a Christian, death is not the worst evil. Sin is worse. Cowardice is worse. Dishonor and betrayal are worse. Default of responsibility is worse. Loss of freedom is worse. Valiant Christians and Jews in Communist countries have proved anew that freedom is more precious than life itself. The American Republic was born with the battlecry, "Give me liberty or give me death," and we all are the beneficiaries of the sacrifices made by our nation's patriots.

Every individual and every nation has the inalienable right of self-defense. An individual may choose not to exercise that right, but individuals and nations who have the responsibility for the defense of others may not default on that responsibility. Jesus said, "Whosoever shall smite thee on thy right cheek, turn to him the other also." But Jesus certainly did *not* say that, if a man smites your wife or child on the right cheek, stand aside and let him smite the left cheek. Nor did Jesus say or imply that governments should "turn the other cheek" in the face of an invading army. One may accept nonviolence for himself, but to hide behind nonviolence when you have family and others to protect who are under your care would be the act of a coward. . . .

The Folly of False Hopes

We recognize that, twenty years ago, the United States embarked upon a remarkable course of independent intiatives to reduce some of the gravest dangers of nuclear war and to encourage a constructive Soviet response. By independent initiatives, we mean carefully chosen limited steps which the United States took for a defined period of time, seeking to elicit a comparable step from the Soviet Union.

At the time of the Cuban Missile Crisis in 1962, according to our President, our U.S. strategic superiority over the Soviets was eight-to-one. In the two decades since then, the United States scrapped more than 2,000 strategic bombers plus plans for building the B-70 and then the B-1, cancelled the plans to build a second thousand Minuteman missiles, scrapped three-fourths of our multi-megaton missiles, (the Atlas and Titan I missiles), cancelled our powerful 24-megaton bomb, scrapped all U.S. intermediate and medium-range missiles, and scrapped the anti-ballistic missile at Grand Forks on the day it became operative.

The result is that, as described by President Reagan, the Soviet Union now has "an increasing, overwhelming advantage. They now enjoy a superiority on the order of six-to-one." He added, "The Soviets' great edge is one in which they could absorb our retaliatory blow and hit us again." Nothing the United States could ever do in terms of weapons-building would be as destabilizing to world peace as the massive Soviet buildup of nuclear weapons.

Garner, *The Washington Times*. Reprinted with permission.

Since no appropriate response has been forthcoming from the Soviet Union, the United States must recognize the folly of independent initiatives and consider ourselves no longer bound by the steps we have previously taken to show our good faith. To engage in further fruitless initiatives would foolishly endanger our nation because, as President Reagan stated on November 11, "Peace is a product of strength, not weakness; of facing reality, not false hopes."

The United States is also conspicuous for its initiatives in addressing the absolute poverty in which millions live today. The United States is unique in having given billions of dollars in foreign aid paid by the taxes of hard-working Americans and sent to more than a hundred countries throughout the world. But we should be mindful, as President Reagan said on November 11, "The first and primary responsibility of our federal government is national security." . . .

Peace movements usually send bad signals. . . . If Soviet leaders think that a pacifist movement is growing in America, they will try to push us first with words and then with weapons.

History affords us many examples of peace movements starting wars. The weapons-freeze movement of the 1930s, cluminating in the Munich ("peace in our time") Agreement, stopped the arms race in the peaceful countries (England and Europe), but promoted the arms race in the warlike countries (Nazi Germany and Japan). In the Kellogg-Briand Treaty signed in 1928, 63 nations solemnly outlawed war; the treaty merely encouraged aggressors to attack. The peace movement of the 1930s *caused* World War II.

The Soviet nuclear arsenal presents a question of conscience we may not evade. It is time we face the truth that the real danger to world peace is not nuclear weapons, but Soviet possession of nuclear weapons combined with their belief that the American response will be weak in spirit and insufficient in weapons. . . .

We are called upon to express our loyalty to the deepest values we cherish: peace with freedom and justice. Our national goals must be measured against that standard. We know that nuclear weapons cannot threaten the sovereignty of God or of God's creation, but that nuclear weapons in the hands of the Soviets can threaten the survival of Christian civilization. . . .

From our faith, we seek to provide hope and strength to all those who seek to live in freedom to love and obey God. Those who have the virtue of hope can live with danger without being

overwhelmed by it. Those who have hope have the ability to struggle against obstacles even when they appear larger than life, because they know they enjoy God's love. It is our belief in the risen Christ which sustains us in confronting the awesome challenge of Soviet nuclear superiority. . . .

We pray that our nation will have both the will and the weapons to defend Western civilization against its greatest threat. We pray that our President and Congress will have the wisdom to cope with their awesome responsibilities. We ask God's help that America will continue to be the defender of all those who seek to love and serve the Lord.

a basic reading and thinking skill

Determining Militarism

Is the United States a militarized society? Two quick – and contradictory – answers can be given to this question. The "yes" answer is usually based on a few pieces of evidence; military expenditures is the one most often cited. The "no" answer rests on the fact that a civilian is Commander-in-Chief of our armed forces and that another civilian, the Secretary of Defense, exercises direct authority over the administration of these forces. . . .

Neither of the answers, of course, is satisfactory. I suspect that what must be done is to treat this question as a genuine query. That means we must let our answer develop out of an understanding of the meaning of the key term, "a militarized society," and out of an examination and critical analysis of the contemporary American experience to determine whether our experience fits the definition of such a society.

The following seem to be major characteristics of a militarized society:

(1) A militarized society is an authoritarian society. Free expression is a threat, dissent cannot be tolerated, and disobedience is met with swift repression.

(2) In a militarized society, stability is a cardinal virtue. Questions of social justice and human rights, when they are not altogether ignored, are viewed with sour suspicion because they cannot be entertained, even abstractly, without at least implying that in certain circumstances stability is not a virtue but a vice.

(3) The militarized society is a fearful society. The ultimate justification for a militarized society is that it is surrounded by enemies. In such an atmosphere, human trust withers, paranoia becomes a national disease, and it is never possible to have too many weapons.

(4) The militarized society is a self-righteous society. It regards its motives as the purest, its values as unquestionable, its ideals as unsurpassable. When it wages war or intervenes in the affairs of another people, it is sure it does so only to protect these qualities or enable others to enjoy them.

(5) In a militarized society, the military is not a means to an end, it is the end itself. Whatever is good for the military is good for society. Military logic is the national philosophy.

(6) A militarized society gives to the military the highest priority in

Based on Donald McDonald's article "Militarism in America," *The Center Magazine*, January 1970. Excerpt used with permission of *The Center Magazine*, a publication of the Robert Maynard Hutchins Center for the Study of Democratic Institutions.

claims on the national resources. In practice, the military consumes the lion's share of the government's revenues from taxes on the people; a substantial part of what is left over is spent to placate a restless people and to repress those who will not be placated.

(7) A militarized society has an unchallengeable claim on the lives of its young men. Conscription into military service becomes a natural–and, in time, almost an unnoticed–part of the political and social landscape.

(8) In a militarized society, the military are beyond effective criticism and control. The institutions that ordinarily exercise such critical control–legislative bodies, courts, the press, universities, churches–are silenced, ignored, or drawn into acquiescence.

(9) In a militarized society, deception is accepted as a normal fact of life. Foreign and domestic espionage, sabotage, subversion, and other para-military activities are carefully cultivated within the military; these have the twofold effect of keeping the enemy off balance and one's own citizens ignorant and therefore unable to ask critical questions.

(10) A militarized society perceives most political problems as military problems and the militarized solution is, therefore, the only realistic solution. The options confronting such a society in a world community are determined and defined by the military. Civilian policymakers who consider other options do so at the risk of being labeled "soft-headed" if not "disloyal."

(11) In a militarized society, the economy is dependent on the military. The military constitutes the single biggest "industry" and its dissolution would be as catastrophic for the nation as the dismantling of the single industry in a one-industry town.

(12) The militarized society is a sterile society. Because it turns human and material resources into instruments of death and consequently neglects problems concerned with the quality of life, and because, in the process, it either suppresses or buys off with enormous rewards of money, prestige, and power the possibility of divergent views and voices, the militarized society deprives itself of the life-quickening energies of its artists and its philosophers, its critics and saints, its youth with their idealism, and its elders with their wisdom and experience. The result is sterility, emptiness, barrenness.

(13) The militarized society is a barbaric society. The barbarian is not necessarily covered with blood, nor does he have to wear a military uniform. In a technologized military society, it is possible for decent people to perform tasks at drawing boards and in laboratories that will insure the death of hundreds of thousands of people halfway around the world; it is possible for pilots and technicians, pressing buttons and switching on computers, to complete the killing process without seeing the faces of those they are killing. Militarization inevitably makes one indifferent about taking human life. A technologized militarization simply makes it easier and less painful to cultivate that indifference.

If the above is an accurate profile of a militarized society, the question is: To what extent is it matched by the contemporary American experience?

In a discussion group or individually, reflect on the viewpoints in this book and your other knowledge about American society. Then for each of the above listed characteristics of a militaristic society, give the US a rating from 0 (not at all true of the US) to 10 (absolutely true of the US). Try to base your rating on concrete evidence.

Finally, average your ratings. According to your analysis, *Is America a Militaristic Society?*

Is Military Spending Harmful?

"Over the last several decades military spending has been the predominant cause of the deterioration of the U.S. economy."

Military Spending Is Destroying the Economy

Lloyd Dumas

Lloyd Dumas is associate professor of political economy and economics at the University of Texas, Dallas. He is a member of the Nuclear Weapons Control Steering Committee of the American Association for the Advancement of Science. Professor Dumas believes that military spending in the past few decades has had a disastrous impact on the U.S. economy. In the following viewpoint, which appeared as an essay in the anthology, *Waging Peace*, Professor Dumas explains why military spending is harmful. He claims there is no economic reason the U.S. cannot convert from military to civilian spending.

As you read, consider the following questions:

1. What four major reasons does the author cite to support his claim that defense spending is destroying the U.S. economy?
2. How does Mr. Dumas suggest the destruction of the U.S. economy can be stopped?
3. Do you agree or disagree with the author's analysis of the U.S. economy?

"The Military Albatross: How Arms Spending Is Destroying the Economy" by Lloyd Dumas in WAGING PEACE, edited by Jim Wallis. Copyright © 1982 by Sojourners. By permission of Harper & Row, Publishers, Inc.

I believe that over the last several decades military spending has been the predominant cause of the deterioration of the U.S. economy, which has, in turn, been largely responsible for our simultaneously high unemployment and inflation. There are four major reasons why this is true.

The first reason is the economic nature of military goods; the second is the nature of military procurement; the third, the balance of payments problem; and the fourth, the effect on civilian technological progress.

The Economic Nature of Military Goods

Whatever else you say about military goods, they have no economic usefulness. They cannot be worn, eaten, or lived in; they make no direct contribution to the material standard of living. Nor do they contribute to an economy's capacity to produce goods and services which do contribute to the standard of living, as do products like industrial machinery and factory buildings.

People who produce military goods and services are, however, paid like everyone else, and the money they receive will be spent by the employees on consumer goods or by the business firms on industrial goods. But these people do not produce a corresponding supply of the consumer or industrial goods which would absorb their money. Taxes have not been raised enough to offset this excess spending power, and inflation has resulted.

Military Contract Practices

The second reason relates to military contract practices. Since World War II, these contracts have in practice become "cost plus," which means that the contractor gets paid whatever it costs to produce plus some amount for profit. The higher the cost, then, the higher the revenues. So contractors interested in bringing more money into the firm simply produce inefficiently, that is, at high cost.

Motivated by this kind of incentive system and backed by a very rich customer, the Department of Defense, these firms have bid resource prices up in order to get the resources they needed. That bidding up of resource prices has contributed to the inflation rate. More importantly, though, the purchasing power of the military industry has enabled it to preempt important parts of key economic resources from the civilian sector.

The Balance of Payments

The third reason is the situation surrounding the balance of payments. From 1893 until 1970, the U.S. had a yearly balance of trade surplus, which meant that exports were greater in value

Reagan Engineering!

Reprinted by permission of *The Daily World.*

than imports. If that had been the only thing going on in the United States' international economic interactions, the U.S. dollar would now be the strongest currency in the world. We know that hasn't happened. The United States' balance of payments has been in deficit for quite a long time. Why?

During the 20 years from 1955 to 1974, U.S. military expenditures abroad alone were 10 percent greater than the entire balance of trade surplus. So the outflow of dollars related to the

support of military establishments and military foreign aid helped to destroy what would otherwise have been a positive balance of payments for the United States.

The pressure generated by the balance of payments deficit is first an inflationary pressure. When the dollar is worth less in exchange for, say, the Swiss franc, a product whose price in Swiss francs has not changed becomes more expensive to U.S. consumers. The United States now imports a great many of its important industrial commodities, including oil and steel. By having to pay more for these imported goods, the U.S. is feeding rising costs into its economic system at its base.

The balance of trade has also turned against the United States in the last few years because the competitive ability of U.S. industry has declined as a result of the technological retardation of U.S. civilian industry, which is in turn a direct result of the military emphasis in the economy. Blaming the non-competitiveness of U.S. industry on the high wages of U.S. labor is nonsense. U.S. wages have been higher than wages in most of the rest of the world for 50 to 100 years, and until very recently the U.S. had no particular difficulty in competing in world markets.

The problem is that large numbers of engineers and scientists are required for the design and manufacture of military products. Estimates of the fraction of all U.S. engineers and scientists engaged in military and military-related work range from about 30 percent to about 50 percent. Pulling this many of them out of civilian work has devastating effects on the rate of civilian technological progress.

Civilian Technological Progress

Technological progress is critical to an economy's ability to offset the rising cost of inputs; that is, as wages, fuel prices, and the costs of raw materials rise, the only way product prices can be held down is to find more efficient ways of producing.

Technological progress is the result of setting engineers and scientists to work on particular problems to solve those problems and develop improved techniques. A large fraction of the engineers and scientists in this country have been working on military-related problems and looking for military applications and solutions, and that's exactly what they've found.

The U.S. is probably the most technologically advanced producer of nuclear submarines, ICBMs, etc., in the world. But when it comes to things like building trolley cars or better railroad cars or better housing, or even finding better techniques

117

for producing steel, the U.S. is not as advanced as some other countries.

Deterioration of civilian technological progress has meant that much of U.S. industry has lost the ability to offset higher labor, fuel, and materials costs, which are passed along to consumers in the form of higher prices. This process has progressively priced U.S. industries out of world markets, and led to a worsening in the balance of trade. It has also priced U.S industries out of the domestic markets.

In addition, engineering and scientific educational institutions have oriented their curricula toward training people for the available jobs. Military technology is highly specialized. It is so much at the frontiers of knowledge that it requires many people, each of whom is an expert in a very small area. This overspecialization is carried through into curricula, and now even the people who have been graduated from our major engineering schools, but who do not go into defense work, have not necessarily had the most appropriate kind of training for work in civilian technological development.

For example, in 1974 I met the president of an energy consulting firm which advises businesses in conserving energy. In 1974 his business was booming, and he wanted to hire more engineers to take care of this additional business. He put an ad in *The New York Times*.

He told me later that he thought he could have built a spacecraft with the people who applied for the jobs. The master designer of the solar panels on one of the major satellite systems asked for work. But my friend couldn't find anyone in that whole group who knew anything about the design or even the operation of an industrial boiler. In fact, one fellow said to him, "You mean they still use boilers in industry?" He finally got the energy engineers he wanted by importing them from Britain.

Clearly, the non-competitiveness of U.S industry due to this technological retardation has not only generated inflation, but also unemployment. When U.S. industries lose markets, U.S. workers lose jobs.

The Solution:
Conversion from Military to Civilian Orientation

Now, the question is what we do about this. A revitalization of U.S. industry is required, which takes a piece-by-piece conversion of U.S. industry from a military to a civilian orientation. This means putting serious money, labor, and technological resources into civilian activity.

How is this done? The first step is to begin contingency planning at all defense facilities (whether they are military bases or production facilities) for alternate, non-military work for the people involved there.

Such a plan requires knowledge of the local situation: who is at the facility in terms of engineers, scientists, and production workers, what their skills are, what equipment is available, and what advantages the site has.

For instance, it would not make much sense for a manufacturing firm that deals with large equipment, such as an aerospace firm which would do a lot of metalworking, to convert to the production of deodorants. It would make more sense to talk about converting to the production of railroad cars or housing modules which would involve the same basic mix of skills.

The next steps are feasibility studies and studies of possible product markets. Probably some people at the firm will have to be retrained and some reoriented; other people will have to be brought in and perhaps others moved elsewhere. Provisions for the interim financial support of these people have to be made.

Conversion for production workers on the whole is not a big problem. Their skills have not generally been overspecialized to military industry. But engineers, scientists, and managers are more problematic.

I indicated before that military production, research, and design requires an extraordinary degree of specialization. It also requires very little attention to the cost implications of design. The particular design of a product significantly influences the cost of making it. Military engineers haven't had to worry about those costs, since the government has paid whatever was required; but civilian markets will not pay any price for a product.

As a result, it becomes necessary for those engineers and scientists to de-specialize so that they have a broader view of the design problem which enables them to trade off one part against another to keep the cost down. Secondly, they have to have cost sensitivity, to know the cost implications of their designs.

Managers who operate in military-industrial firms operate in a different world than managers in civilian industry. For example, the military-industrial firm's manager doesn't have to know anything about marketing a product in terms of surveying consumers, doing market-feasibility studies, or running a mass media ad campaign. These firms' managers have only one customer, the Department of Defense. What they have to know are

the Armed Services Procurement Regulations, the procurement people, and the congresspeople involved. Yet this knowledge has no relationship to what is needed to market a new detergent, piece of furniture, record, or anything else in civilian industry.

With respect to cost sensitivity, that same distinction exists. In military industry, the cost question is not the prime one. In civilian industry, holding cost *down* is one of the primary functions of management. Managers must understand how to do that.

Economics of the Arms Race

Since World War II, the United States has spent over two trillion dollars for military purposes. We spent almost one trillion dollars during the 1970's alone. The present administration now proposes to spend more than 1.5 trillion dollars for military purposes during the next five years. If this program is carried out, we can expect:

Our scarce finite resources will become more scarce.

A worsening of our high interest-rate problem.

Federal deficits that will be mind-boggling.

Many low-income people, as well as the sick, aged, and the unemployed, will find their economic situation becoming more desperate.

Corporations with military contracts will make millions of dollars of additional profits, while low- and middle-income groups will be seriously hurt.

As a nation, we will be less secure.

John C. Davis, "Economics of the Arms Race," *The Churchman*, April-May 1983.

So successful conversion at any given facility requires the retraining and reorientation of the management personnel. If retraining is not done in advance, it must be done in process, and that delays everything and makes it more expensive. For example, Boeing is now producing trolley cars in its Vertol Division. But Boeing didn't retrain in advance. Instead it threw out a good part of the military management in the Vertol Division and brought in management from its civilian divisions. Then it sent its engineers on a world tour to learn how to produce trolley cars in places where they are still made. (There hasn't been one produced in the United States for 25 years.)

As a result, Boeing is in a terrible financial mess with respect to its trolley car production. It signed a fixed-price contract with Chicago and with Boston, and those cities are not the Depart-

ment of Defense; they are holding Boeing to these fixed prices, though costs have gone way above the prices. Boeing is losing a fortune. If reorientation had been done in advance, there would have been no reason to throw out the managers; and Boeing would have found itself capable of meeting those contracts or, at least, signing realistic ones: It would have known what it was doing and how to do it.

Conclusion

There is no economic reason why conversion of military facilities to civilian use cannot take place. There is no question of whether enough jobs can be generated. More than enough things that do contribute to the economy need doing in this country and around the world. Labor is one of our most valuable resources. That is not the problem.

The problem is, first of all, developing the political will and, secondly, understanding the economics of this transitional period, in order that the conversion of military facilities to civilian operation can be done smoothly and effectively without seriously disrupting the lives of the people involved, without throwing them out of work until they happen to find a job somewhere that may not even use their skills.

The benefits of carrying out such a conversion are substantial. It is no longer just an idealist's dream or a peacenik's vision. It is the only real hope of revitalizing the U.S. economy on a permanent and enduring basis, of getting us out of the economic mess in which we find ourselves.

"In FY-1984, defense spending will be 28.1% of the federal budget. . . . Twenty years ago 41.7% of the budget went to defense. . . . So defense is certainly not taking more than its fair share."

U.S. Must Respond to Soviet Spending

Caspar W. Weinberger

In the following viewpoint, Secretary Weinberger continues his defense of military spending begun in the first chapter. He claims the Reagan Administration's defense spending program is not only necessary but well thought out. The Secretary's viewpoint, originally presented as a speech before The Conservative Political Action Conference in February 1983, argues that to cut defense spending for political or economic reasons may mean the sacrifice of America's freedom.

As you read, consider the following questions:

1. According to Secretary Weinberger, what emphasis are the Soviets putting on their military spending?
2. What three point strategy has the Reagan administration devised to respond to Soviet military spending?
3. Why does Secretary Weinberger claim that "defense is certainly not taking more than its fair share," when referring to the U.S. 1984 fiscal year budget?

Caspar Weinberger, "Remarks before the Conservative Political Action Conference," Sheraton Washington Hotel, Washington, DC, February 18, 1983. News release by the Office of Assistant Secretary of Defense (Public Affairs), Washington, DC 20301.

I have heard some senators and congressmen tell me that we must cut defense spending in order to reduce the deficit or unemployment, or to be fair to other programs.

What I have been telling them is that cutting defense won't reduce the deficit dollar for dollar. A one dollar defense cut only provides a reduction in the deficit of about 50 cents. And for every $1B cut from defense, 35,000 jobs are lost. Finally, defense has already taken its fair share of cuts. We have reduced by more than half the increase to the Carter budget planned by President Reagan just two years ago. Yet, none of those are reasons to spend defense dollars – only the threat provides that rationale.

We all understand the value of stable investments in maintaining a strong and profitable business. Even the leaders of an industry know that if their competitors continuously invest more than they do, their competitors will eventually outproduce them. This is precisely what has happened between the United States and its chief competitor, the Soviet Union. Only in this case, the stakes are not shares of a market but are much higher – the preservation of peace.

Defense Spending Dropped During the 1970's

Let me take a moment to discuss what had been happening before President Reagan arrived in Washington. Throughout the 1970s, defense spending had been dropping steadily – falling about 20 percent in real terms – while federal transfer payments rose by about 122 percent. During the decade, the United States spent an average of 5.9 percent of GNP on defense – far less than the 8-9% spent during the 1950s and 1960s.

Meanwhile the Soviets were spending an enormous amount on defense. Despite the Soviets' sluggish economic situation and food shortages, the Soviet military now consumes an estimated 15 percent of GNP. And most of that is spent on modern weapons. While usually about 50% of our defense budget covers personnel costs (it is about 44% this year) the Soviets spend only about 16% for personnel. The rest is spent on military hardware. That says a lot about the differences of our two societies.

By 1980, total Soviet military investment was nearly double ours. When we analyze that investment comparison more closely we can see where the Soviets are putting their emphasis. During 1980 and 1981 their investment in strategic nuclear forces was about three times higher than ours. For conventional forces it was about 50 percent higher, and for research and development

it was twice our rate.

As you well know, investments do not tell the whole story. What is important is the output – the tanks, planes, ships, missiles, and other military hardware the Soviets produce and deploy. And here the divergences between the United States and the Soviet Union are just as disturbing. During the period 1974-1982, for example, they out-produced the United States in practically every category of weapons: building almost 3 times more tanks, twice as many tactical combat aircraft, six times more ICBMs, and 16 times more nuclear submarines.

President Reagan designed his defense program to begin restoring a military balance with the Soviets. But even with his increases to the defense budget, we still fall far short of offsetting Soviet production of weapons. For example, the FY-1984 budget provides for 720 tanks while the Soviets' average annual production for their own forces is over 1,900 tanks. The Defense Department is requesting funds for 188 artillery pieces and rocket launchers; the Soviets' annual production is over seven times greater. In addition, they produce on the average twice as many combat aircraft and three times more warships than President Reagan has requested in his budget. And still there are those who say that the budget should be cut. . . .

The Soviet Buildup and the Reagan Strategy

We do, however, recognize that it is not necessary to match the Soviets tank for tank or aircraft for aircraft. Our intention is to regain an effective deterrent against either Soviet conventional or nuclear aggression. Other factors besides quantitative comparisons affect the military balance. One of the most important of these is that the Soviets have matched their military buildup with military and political expansion into strategically important areas far from the Soviet periphery.

The Soviet Union now has:
- Acquired security and cooperative agreements worldwide.
- Undertaken massive arms deliveries to Third World countries – double the amount we supplied from 1977-1981.
- Acquired Cuban, East German and/or Libyan military proxies in Central America and Africa.
- Greatly increased its power projection capabilities.
- Expanded its overflight and access rights to operating bases in key parts of the world.
- Occupied Afghanistan.
- Continues to intimidate and threaten Poland.

To cope with all those unsettling threats to peace posed by the Soviet military buildup and expansion, the Reagan administration formulated a strategy based firmly on three enduring principles that have worked in the past:

First, *our strategy is defensive.* The United States does not start fights, which means we cede to our potential adversaries the advantage of surprise, and the opportunity to pick the time and place of conflict. As a result, our forces must be maintained in a high state of readiness; our command, control, and communications and intelligence capabilities must be flexible and enduring; and we must have the capability to mobilize rapidly.

Second, *our strategy is to deter war.* For this we need a strong and survivable nuclear and conventional force posture designed to convince any potential adversary that the cost of aggression would be too high to justify an attack.

Third, *should deterrence fail, our strategy is to restore peace on terms favorable to the U.S.* For this we need mobile, flexible, and sustainable forces with capabilities that can counter the increasingly sophisticated forces that would be deployed against us.

Defense Spending Has Fallen

The fact is that in the past few decades we have seen a dramatic shift in how we spend the taxpayer's dollar. Back in 1955, payments to individuals took up only about 20% of the Federal budget. For nearly three decades, these payments steadily increased, and this year will account for 49% of the budget. By contrast, in 1955 defense took up more than half of the Federal budget. By 1980, this spending had fallen to a low of 23%. Even with the increase that I am requesting this year, defense will still amount to only 28% of the budget.

President Ronald Reagan in an address to the nation on March 23, 1983.

When the Reagan administration took office there were serious gaps between the existing strategy and the forces then available to carry it through. Our forces had to be made ready to fight immediately, should conflict be forced upon us. We also needed to begin long-term improvements to our defense posture so that we would be prepared to meet threats that might arise in the future. Confronting this "double-duty" had tremendous consequences for the defense budget.

The Progress We Have Made

The first problems that we addressed were the poor state of

readiness and our personnel shortcomings. We had to attend to them because we were concerned that our forces were unprepared to respond if a crisis were to arise. To obtain the necessary funds, President Reagan submitted a supplemental to the FY '81 budget and amended the FY '82 budget. Congress approved the President's request and we used those funds to buy spare parts to restore our equipment to operational condition, to pay for fuel and ammunition for training, and, most importantly, to restore adequate levels of military compensation to keep the all-volunteer force from collapsing.

Our readiness investments worked. Today the services are all recruiting more than their quota of recruits and all have waiting lists. The proportion of high school graduates we recruited has risen almost 26% in the past two years. The number of eligible servicemen and women choosing to reenlist has also risen from 55% two years ago to almost 70% in the past year.

Pay has not been the only incentive for our young men and women choosing to stay in the service. They appreciate the fact that now they have more tools and spare parts to keep their equipment in operating condition. And they now know that they are receiving the training that they require to do their jobs well. For example, by next year air crews for air force tactical fighter and attack aircraft will average about 20 hours of flight training per month, compared to the only 13 hours per month they received a few years ago. The Army is also now able to give new recruits an additional week of basic training.

Along with readiness, the Reagan administration also emphasized sustainability – the ability of our forces to continue fighting for as long as they need to. Stocks of supplies and ammunition had fallen to precariously low levels. President Reagan obtained passage of an amendment to the FY 1982 budget that increased sustainability funding by about 30%. This increased emphasis has continued through the FY-83 and FY-84 budgets. Improvements in sustainability are slower and less visible than readiness improvements, but our war reserve stocks are gradually being replenished. For example, when the FY-84 budget is executed, our sustainability will have been increased by about 25% over that inherited from the previous administration.

While we were paying the bills for readiness and sustainability, we were also making some long-term investments in modernizing our forces. We knew that the dividends from our modernization investments would not be apparent for several years, but we had to take measures quickly if we were to offset

the increasing sophistication of Soviet weapons and meet our global commitments. For example, the previous administration had halted funding for the Air Force's KC-10 transports and the Navy's amphibious lift ships. Yet, with the threats to the oil fields in the Middle East, strategic mobility had taken on great importance. We restored funds to those programs and we rejuvenated several other programs that had been budgeted at low and inefficient rates.

We also had to attend to our strategic forces. During the past decade, the United States essentially had a unilateral freeze in nuclear forces. In 1970 we began replacing the Minuteman I ICBM and deployed the Poseidon missile. After that we did not deploy a single new system until we began deploying the Trident I missile in 1979. During the same period, the Soviet Union tested and deployed three new ICBMs. three new SLBMs, and five improved SLBMs.

Because we have neglected our strategic forces for so long, we must modernize all three parts of the triad at the same time. In some areas we have made a good start – our first B-1 bombers will be flying soon; the first two Trident submarines have been commissioned. In the case of the all-important land-based leg of the triad, we have been delayed by the unwillingness of the Con-

THAT REAGAN MANIAC CAN'T GET TO US IN HERE!!

FREEZE

Reprinted by permission: Tribune Company Syndicate, Inc.

gress to accept the basing recommended by the President for the MX. The MX is a vital part of our strategic recovery because it is the only missile virtually ready for deployment, that can deter war on us. In appointing a bi-partisan panel to present a recommendation for the peacekeeper, President Reagan has shown his determination to maintain the triad as the keystone of our deterrence in the future.

The Price of Defense

In short, then, that is a quick report on how the Reagan defense program is addressing the problems we found two years ago. There has been progress, but there still is a long way to go.

The FY-84 defense budget that President Reagan recently presented to Congress assures that we remain on a steady course in restoring America's defenses – and it does it in a reasonable and prudent way. While a budget of $273B is indeed substantial, it still takes a far smaller share of our national treasure than budgets of earlier years. In FY-1984, defense spending will be 28.1% of the federal budget – as compared to 47.3% for transfer payments. Twenty years ago 41.7% of the budget went to defense and only 26.6% to transfer payments. So defense is certainly not taking more than its fair share.

Even so, in the coming months we will hear calls from those who refuse to face reality that defense should be cut for political or economic reasons. They have forgotten how important freedom is to the well-being of our nation, and they have ignored the lessons of history. Speaking of the demise of one of the first truly free societies – Athens – an historian once wrote:

> When the freedom they wished for most was freedom from responsibility, then Athens ceased to be free and was never free again.

Let us never succumb to the same temptation to think that America can have freedom from that most essential responsibility – the responsibility to maintain the defenses necessary to protect our liberties. If we want to preserve peace with freedom, we are going to have to complete the job we began two years ago. That is the only wise and prudent course.

"Every $1 billion transferred from purchases by consumers to purchases by the Pentagon caused a net loss of 12,000 jobs in industry and commerce."

Pentagon Spending Costs Jobs

Employment Research Associates

Employment Research Associates (ERA) describes itself as "an independent, non-profit, economic consulting firm which specializes in analyzing the impact of government policies in the U.S. economy." In the past few years ERA has published a number of booklets (including *Bombs or Bread* and *Bankrupting America*) discussing the harmful impact of military spending on the U.S. economy. The following viewpoint, excerpted from the booklet *The Price of the Pentagon*, claims that military spending has a negative impact on the U.S. economy, both in terms of jobs created and purchasing power generated.

As you read, consider the following questions:

1. ERA claims that in 1981 money spent by the Pentagon cost the U.S. the loss of 1,520,000 jobs. What evidence is presented to support this claim?
2. Why does ERA also claim that defense spending has seriously harmed the advance of civilian industrial technology?
3. What recommendations does ERA make?

Employment Research Associates, "The Price of the Pentagon: The Industrial and Commercial Impact of the 1981 Military Budget," 2nd Edition. Employment Research Associates, 474 Hollister Building, Lansing, MI 48944.

Our taxpayers and our businesses pay a high price for the Pentagon. It is high in terms of money. It is high in terms of jobs.

In 1981, when the military budget was $154 billion, it caused a net loss of 1,520,000 jobs to the industrial and commercial base of the United States.[1]

This was a net loss of jobs. All of the jobs generated in industry and commerce through the purchase of goods and services by the Pentagon were taken into consideration. This figure was then compared with the number of jobs which would have been created if the taxpayers had spent the money on their normal needs: food, housing, clothing, cars, medical care and other goods and services.

If this money had not been going from the taxpayer to the Pentagon, 3,284,000 jobs in industry, agriculture, mining, commerce, and services would have been generated by consumer purchases. The Pentagon's 1981 expenditures for nuclear weapons, aircraft, submarines, and other goods and services, generated 1,764,000 jobs. Therefore, the net loss to our industrial and commercial base in 1981 alone was 1,520,000 jobs.

In 1981, when consumers spent $1 billion on goods and services, 38,000 jobs were created. The Pentagon's spending the same sum on the procurement of goods and services generated 26,000 jobs.

Therefore, every $1 billion transferred from purchases by consumers to purchases by the Pentagon caused a net loss of 12,000 jobs in industry and commerce.

Over 85% of all Americans work in industries or businesses which suffer a net loss of jobs with every rise in the Pentagon's budget. Of the 156 industries studied, only 29 gained jobs when military spending is high.

Basic industries were especially hard hit. Automobile manufacturing suffered a net loss of over 200,000 jobs, basic steel of 35,000 jobs, textile manufacture of 260,000 jobs and construction of 102,000 jobs.

All of these jobs were lost due to diminished consumer spending. It is difficult to visualize what the transference of $154 billion from the taxpayer to the Pentagon means to the average person, the average family. This transfer of funds through

---

1. Total DOD outlays in 1981 were $154 billion. This report is on the impact of military spending upon the U.S. economy. Only purchases and payments made by the military in the U.S. were taken into consideration. (See methodological notes.)

Federal taxes cost the average American family $2,200.[2] This was $2,200 less to spend in 1981 for food, housing, education and all other needs.

This negative job impact is not widely understood. For decades, the Pentagon and its contractors have told Congress and the public that military contracts create jobs. But they have not been equally forthright in discussing the other side of the ledger: the price paid by consumers in lost disposable income, and by businesses in lost sales and investment as a result of

The Net Loss Industries

	JOBS
Agricultural Products and Processed Foods	- 85,000
New Residential Building Construction	- 116,000
Lumber and Wood Products	- 70,000
Textiles and Clothing Manufacture	- 260,000
Newspapers, Periodicals and Book Printing and Publishing	- 31,000
Motor Vehicles	- 206,000
Primary Metal Industries	- 35,000
Fabricated Metals	- 45,000
Transportaion	- 15,000
Retail Trade	- 585,000
Wholesale Trade	- 66,000
Services	- 76,000
Banking, Insurance, and Real Estate	- 184,000

The Net Gain Industries

Ordnance and Guided Missiles	+ 132,000
Aircraft	+ 189,000
Shipbuilding	+ 39,700

financing these military contracts.

This study shows both sides: how many jobs are generated through military procurement, and how many jobs are lost when taxpayers do not have this money to spend on their own needs. It also shows the negative impact of military spending on investment in a number of key industries. The results of the analysis show a severe loss of jobs and income to the hard pressed industrial and commercial base of the United States.

2. Based on a per family figure of 3.37 derived from data in the U.S. *Statistical Abstract, 1981.* Most of this tax money was through direct taxation, some was through indirect taxation.

Introduction

There are two parts to the analysis. First, it had to be determined how many jobs were lost due to diminished consumer spending. Then, the number of jobs generated by all military purchases in the United States were determined, and the results compared.

Data has been developed by the Bureau of Labor Statistics showing how consumers respond to incremental changes in income.[3] Using this data, it was possible to determine exactly which industries were affected as consumer expenditures decreased due to the transference of money from taxpayers to the Pentagon. For instance, a $1 million transfer from consumers to military procurement meant a decrease of $329,000 in the demand for automobiles, $78,000 in the demand for textiles, and $77,000 in the demand for food.

It then had to be determined how this decline in consumer demand affected output and employment in key industrial and commercial sectors of the economy. For this part of the analysis, the Bureau of Labor Statistics Input-Output model of the economy was used.

The Input-Output model shows how a dollar of demand for one industry's product affects output and employment in 156 sectors of the economy, ranging from the production of grains to the production of machine tools to restaurants. For example, a demand for cars has an impact on steel, electrical machinery, coal, hotels and many other sectors of the economy.

The same Input-Output model was then used to determine the changes in industrial and commercial output and employment resulting from military purchases. The negative job impact of the foregone consumer expenditures was then compared to the jobs generated by military purchases.

The results show that a vast array of industries ranging from agriculture to clothing, and from foundries to hospitals suffered a net loss of output and jobs due to military spending.

There are two key reasons for this result. First, the production of military products is more capital intensive than most production for consumer goods. The military makes the bulk of its purchases from contractors who spend more on expensive machinery and less on personnel than the mix of businesses and industries which provide goods and services for consumers.

Second, the industries and businesses from which the military makes its purchases have a higher rate of inflation than the

---

3. Elasticity of demand data developed by Bureau of Labor Statistics.

inflation prevailing in civilian industries. This means that a dollar spent by the military stimulates less industrial activity than if the dollar was spent by the consumer. . . .

The Undermined Economy

The decline in consumer purchases and the resulting loss of jobs are only part of the price that we pay for Pentagon spending. For three decades, sustained high Pentagon budgets have choked off investment in research and development, new civilian technology, and in new factories and industrial equipment.

As a result, the United States has experienced dramatic declines in key industries, such as steel, machinery, consumer electronics and textiles. This is a major reason for the deterioration of our industrial centers and ever-rising unemployment that we are experiencing today.

The preeminence given to military industry and technology over the last three decades has had a delayed but serious impact upon the civilian industrial economy. In stark contrast to the enormous sums allotted over the years to military technology, civilian technology has been starved for capital and thus for talent as people neither train for nor enter fields where they are unable to find employment.

Over the last two decades, between 30% and 50% of the U.S. scientists and engineers have been working on military and space contracts.[4] This has meant that great pool of talent has not been available to work on civilian commercial designs and applications of new technology. There is no mystery why our economic competitors have surpassed us in production advances in steel, autos, machine tools and electronics. They have captured markets in which we were once world leaders.

Financing the military has siphoned a tremendous amount of investment capital out of the civilian economy. People have little sense of the magnitude of this drain. During the 1960's and 1970's, the Pentagon spent more money *every single year* than the after tax profits of all U.S. corporations combined.

Caspar Weinberger, before he became Secretary of Defense, clearly saw the danger of overspending on the military. Speaking at a seminar at the American Enterprise Institute he said,

> The identification of a threat to security does not automatically require an expenditure in the defense budget to neutralize it . . . . The defense budget, in short, must be seen not only in terms of what we must defend ourselves against, but what we have to defend. The more

4. Melman, Seymour, *Pentagon Capitalism*, McGraw-Hill, 1970, pg. 89, and Employment Research Associates.

we take from the common wealth for its defense, the smaller it becomes.[5]

The Double Competition

The growing role of the Pentagon and the military contractors in our economy has forced American business into a competition on two fronts – at home and abroad.

First, civilian businesses must compete with the Pentagon and with military contractors for scarce talent, and for limited supplies of machinery and equipment. Competition with military industry has forced businesses either to pay a higher price for investment or to do without.

Civilian firms must also compete for investment funds. When the Federal government borrows to finance the Pentagon budget, capital is drawn from the civilian economy.

President Reagan's former chief economist, Murray Weidenbaum said that the record expansion in the nation's military budget has contributed to "horrendous deficits."[6] This drives up interest rates. Military contractors themselves also enter the money markets to borrow capital for the production of military hardware, giving an additional boost to interest rates. The resulting high interest rates increase the cost to businesses of borrowing to make investments.

In the fall of 1980, the Pentagon asked five major forecasting firms – Data Resources, Inc., Wheaton Econometrics Forecasting Associates, Merrill-Lynch Economics, Evans Economics and Chase Econometrics – to predict the impact of increases in the military budget. All agreed that the most dangerous problem was slower investment as a result of increased federal borrowing to cover military increases.[7]

Disadvantaged by these business conditions at home, civilian firms must then face a second competition. They must compete for markets against Japanese, German and other European firms, all of which have easy access to their own scientists, engineers and capital. Because our investment in civilian industry has lagged due to Pentagon competition, we have been severely handicapped in facing growing competition from abroad.

Three Decades of Diminished Investment

The decline of our industrial infrastructure makes it

5. *The Washington Post*, August 31, 1982, pg. A2.

6. *Detroit Free Press*, August 27, 1982, pg. B1.

7. DeGrasse, Robert, et.al. **The Costs and Consequences of Reagan's Military Build-Up**, Council on Economic Priorities, New York, 1982, pg. 6.

increasingly important to understand the relationship between the loss in investment for civilian industries and high military budgets.

Employment Research Associates did a statistical analysis to quantify the specific impact of military spending upon investment in the following industries: primary metals; stone, clay and glass; rubber; chemicals; paper; lumber; machinery; fabricated metals; motor vehicles; textiles; furniture; publishing; petroleum; apparel; leather; railroads; electrical machinery, and non-electrical machinery.

The results show a significant *negative impact* upon eight of these key industries during the period of analysis, 1953-1980. In only one industry, electrical machinery, did the analysis show a

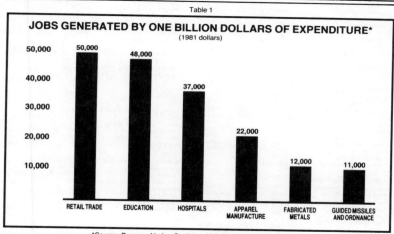

Table 1

JOBS GENERATED BY ONE BILLION DOLLARS OF EXPENDITURE*
(1981 dollars)

*Source: Bureau of Labor Statistics, U.S. Statistical Abstract, 1981.

positive investment impact due to military spending.

For each $1 billion dollars in Pentagon spending, investment in primary metals declined by over $53,000,000, in the textile industry by almost $8,000,000, and in non-electrical machinery by $130,000. These industries, which once formed an important part of the core of the U.S. industrial strength, now stand among those industries suffering the most significant losses, plant closings and loss of jobs.

Military spending in 1981 alone caused these critical industries to suffer a net loss in investment of over $11 billion. The military spending increase during 1982 caused a loss in investment of $13.3 billion; in 1983, the loss will be over $15 billion.

135

Table 2
Job Impact by Category of the Economy

— NET LOSS INDUSTRIES —

	Jobs Foregone Due To Diminished Consumer Expenditures	Jobs Created Through Military Expenditures	Net Job Loss or Gain
AGRICULTURE, FORESTRY AND FISHERIES			
Dairy & poultry products	−12,720	+3,550	−9,170
Meat animals & livestock	−17,060	+6,050	−11,010
Cotton	−12,540	+1,250	−11,290
Food & feed grains	−11,800	+3,710	−8,090
Agricultural products, n.e.c.	−14,110	+5,740	−8,370
Forestry & fishery products	−2,500	+760	−1,740
Agricultural, forestry, & fishery services	−8,300	+3,740	−4,560
MINING			
Iron & ferroalloy ores mining	−2,720	+1,520	−1,200
Copper ore mining	−1,820	+1,580	−240
Nonferrous metal ores mining, except copper	−1,580	+1,490	−90
Coal mining	−6,560	+3,890	−2,670
Crude petroleum & natural gas	−6,490	+5,190	−1,300
Stone & clay mining & quarrying	−2,520	+1,720	−800
Chemical & fertilizer mineral mining	−800	+350	−450
CONSTRUCTION			
Residential construction*	−116,170		−116,170
FOOD AND KINDRED PRODUCTS			
Meat products	−8,560	+3,100	−5,460
Dairy products	−4,190	+950	−3,240
Canned & frozen foods	−7,140	+2,250	−4,890
Grain mill products	−2,730	+720	−2,010
Bakery products	−5,020	+980	−4,040
Sugar	−1,070	+290	−780
Confectionery products	−1,570	+930	−640
Alcoholic beverages	−5,200	+540	−4,660
Soft drinks & flavorings	−3,010	+480	−2,530
Food products, n.e.c.	−3,130	+1,050	−2,080
Tobacco manufacturing	−810	+300	−510
TEXTILES AND APPAREL			
Fabric, yarn, & thread mills	−67,310	+5,660	−61,650
Floor covering mills	−5,510	+310	−5,200
Textile mill products, n.e.c.	−7,300	+2,440	−4,860
Hosiery & knit goods	−29,700	+2,000	−27,700
Apparel	−141,070	+10,900	−130,170
Fabricated textile products, n.e.c.	−32,000	+1,430	−30,570
LUMBER PRODUCTS INCLUDING FURNITURE			
Logging	−5,720	+1,730	−3,990
Sawmills & planing mills	−12,540	+3,280	−9,260
Millwork, plywood & wood products, n.e.c.	−13,100	+4,280	−8,820
Household furniture	−47,400	+1,630	−45,770
Furniture & fixtures, except household	−2,580	+1,500	−1,080
PAPER AND PRINTING			
Paper products	−22,960	+7,490	−15,470
Paperboard	−11,620	+3,850	−7,770
Newspaper printing & publishing	−15,030	+5,830	−9,200
Periodical & book print & publishing	−11,340	+2,390	−8,950
Printing & publishing, n.e.c.	−22,770	+9,950	−12,820
CHEMICALS AND ALLIED PRODUCTS			
Industrial inorganic & organic chemicals	−13,830	+6,030	−7,800

— NET LOSS INDUSTRIES —

	Jobs Foregone Due To Diminished Consumer Expenditures	Jobs Created Through Military Expenditures	Net Job Loss or Gain
(Chemicals and Allied Products continued)			
Agricultural chemicals	−1,250	+520	−730
Chemical products, n.e.c.	−4,040	+2,490	−1,550
Plastic materials & synthetic rubber	−6,120	+2,630	−3,490
Synthetic fibers	−13,650	+1,710	−11,940
Drugs	−2,760	+880	−1,880
Cleaning & toilet preparations	−8,110	+760	−7,350
Paints & allied products	−3,160	+2,180	−980
PETROLEUM			
Petroleum refining & related products	−7,530	+6,340	−1,190
RUBBER AND PLASTIC PRODUCTS			
Tires & inner tubes	−6,610	+1,480	−5,130
Rubber products except tires & tubes	−11,620	+3,280	−8,340
Plastic products	−20,010	+7,810	−12,200
LEATHER PRODUCTS			
Leather tanning & industrial leather	−3,850	+80	−3,770
Leather products including footwear	−41,590	+470	−41,120
STONE, CLAY AND GLASS PRODUCTS			
Glass	−16,870	+3,850	−13,020
Cement & concrete products	−4,000	+2,460	−1,540
Structural clay products	−1,330	+960	−370
Pottery & related products	−4,890	+1,080	−3,810
Stone & clay products, n.e.c.	−6,300	+3,570	−2,730
PRIMARY METAL PRODUCTS			
Blast furnaces & basic steel products	−42,410	+23,700	−18,710
Iron & steel foundries & forgings	−27,660	+11,800	−15,860
Primary copper & copper products	−7,050	+6,400	−650
Primary aluminum & aluminum products	−9,220	+8,680	−540
FABRICATED METAL PRODUCTS			
Metal containers	−3,260	+1,030	−2,230
Heating apparatus & plumbing fixtures	−1,830	+1,440	−390
Screw machine products	−9,400	+6,870	−2,530
Metal stampings	−34,850	+6,170	−28,680
Cutlery, handtools & general hardware	−14,840	+3,550	−11,290
Fabricated metal products, n.e.c.	−15,670	+12,100	−3,570
NON-ELECTRICAL MACHINERY			
Farm machinery	−1,080	+1,050	−30
Special industry machinery	−2,440	+2,010	−430
Nonelectrical machinery, n.e.c.	−15,400	+15,100	−300
Service industry machinery	−6,610	+2,530	−4,080
ELECTRICAL MACHINERY			
Household appliances	−19,730	+1,400	−18,330
Electric lighting & wiring	−9,770	+6,300	−3,470
Radio & television receiving sets	−44,350	+1,520	−42,830
Electrical machinery & equipment, n.e.c.	−11,530	+2,980	−8,550

*Military residential construction is included in Maintenance and Repair Construction.

n.e.c. = not elsewhere counted

Taken from *National Security Record,* May 1983, by The Heritage Foundation.

Job Impact by Category of the Economy (continued)

	Jobs Foregone Due To Diminished Consumer Expenditures	Jobs Created Through Military Expenditures	Net Job Loss or Gain
— NET LOSS INDUSTRIES —			
TRANSPORTATION EQUIPMENT			
Motor vehicles	–215,750	+10,000	–205,750
Railroad equipment	–410	+400	–10
Motorcycles, bicycles & parts	–6,220	+400	–5,820
Transportation equipment, n.e.c.	–3,000	+670	–2,330
INSTRUMENTS AND RELATED PRODUCTS			
Optical & ophthalmic equipment	–10,970	+2,800	–8,170
Watches, clocks, & clock operated devices	–5,570	+1,280	–4,290
MISC. MANUFACTURING INDUSTRIES			
Jewelry & silverware	–6,620	+220	–6,400
Musical instruments & sporting goods	–32,920	+790	–32,130
Manufactured products, n.e.c.	–8,800	+7,350	–1,450
TRANSPORTATION			
Railroad transportation	–21,110	+9,160	–11,950
Local transit & intercity buses	–6,440	+4,860	–1,580
Truck transportation	–33,840	+19,200	–14,640
Pipeline transportation	–500	+400	–100
COMMUNICATIONS			
Radio & television broadcasting	–7,340	+2,820	–4,520
Communications, except radio & television	–35,400	+29,500	–5,900
UTILITIES			
Electric utilities, public & private	–18,260	+13,000	–5,260
Gas utilities, excluding public	–6,850	+4,080	–2,770
Water & sanitary services, excluding public	–3,660	+2,030	–1,630
WHOLESALE AND RETAIL TRADE			
Wholesale trade	–115,250	+49,400	–65,850
Eating & drinking places	–110,640	+44,800	–65,840
Retail trade, except eating & drinking places	–543,060	+24,400	–518,660
FINANCE, INSURANCE AND REAL ESTATE			
Banking	–40,840	+11,900	–28,940
Credit agencies & financial brokers	–94,040	+7,480	–86,560
Insurance	–64,260	+7,240	–57,020
Real estate	–24,800	+13,200	–11,600
SERVICES			
Hotels & lodging places	–114,330	+22,300	–92,030
Personal & repair services	–81,880	+15,700	–66,180
Advertising	–7,020	+2,710	–4,310
Automobile repair	–20,010	+7,530	–12,480
Motion pictures	–10,140	+1,700	–8,440
Amusements & recreation services	–19,100	+2,250	–16,850
Doctors' & dentists' services	–30,700	+30	–30,670
Hospitals	–53,750	+2,480	–51,270
Medical services, except hospitals	–4,200	+300	–3,900
Educational services	–39,370	+31,900	–7,470
GOVERNMENT			
Post office	–21,760	+15,300	–6,460
Federal enterprises, n.e.c.	–6,250	+790	–5,460

	Jobs Foregone Due To Diminished Consumer Expenditures	Jobs Created Through Military Expenditures	Net Job Loss or Gain
— NET LOSS INDUSTRIES —			
(Government continued)			
Local government passenger transit	–2,100	+1,600	–500
State & local government, enterprises, n.e.c.	–12,170	+6,610	–5,560
— NET GAIN INDUSTRIES —			
CONSTRUCTION			
Maintenance & repair construction	–27,200	+41,400	+14,200
LUMBER PRODUCTS INCLUDING FURNITURE			
Wooden containers	–1,400	+1,550	+150
PRIMARY METAL AND FABRICATED METAL PRODUCTS			
Primary nonferrous metals & products, n.e.c.	–5,490	+6,280	+790
Fabricated structural metal products	–4,770	+8,620	+3,850
NON-ELECTRICAL MACHINERY			
Engines, turbines, & generators	–4,430	+7,900	+3,470
Construction, mining & oilfield machinery	–2,070	+2,390	+320
Material handling equipment	–1,010	+2,840	+1,830
Metalworking machinery	–7,340	+16,900	+9,560
General industrial machinery	–9,060	+11,700	+2,640
Computers & peripheral equipment	–1,530	+9,400	+7,870
Typewriters & other office equipment	–740	+930	+190
ELECTRICAL MACHINERY			
Electric transmission equipment	–2,400	+6,090	+3,690
Electrical industrial apparatus	–7,090	+10,000	+2,910
Telephone & telegraph apparatus	–1,300	+3,990	+2,690
Radio & communication equipment	–1,640	+124,000	+122,360
Electronic components	–22,310	+59,400	+37,090
ORDNANCE AND GUIDED MISSILES			
Ordnance	–470	+40,400	+39,930
Complete guided missiles & space vehicles	–140	+92,100	+91,960
TRANSPORTATION EQUIPMENT			
Aircraft	–2,060	+192,000	+189,940
Ship & boat building & repair	–4,850	+44,500	+39,650
INSTRUMENTS AND RELATED PRODUCTS			
Scientific and controlling instruments	–3,260	+19,400	+16,140
Medical & dental instruments	–1,590	+3,420	+1,830
Photographic equipment & supplies	–1,810	+3,150	+1,340
TRANSPORTATION			
Water transportation	–3,800	+13,700	+9,900
Air transportation	–14,840	+17,000	+2,160
Transportation services	–4,670	+5,500	+830
SERVICES			
Business services, n.e.c.	–83,530	+288,000	+204,470
Professional services, n.e.c.	–45,360	+47,500	+2,140
Nonprofit organizations	–15,300	+26,100	+10,800

Net Jobs Lost –1,520,000

The impact of this loss of investment is ominous: declining productivity, the loss of markets at home and abroad, higher unemployment, and a rising balance-of-payments deficit which both weakens the dollar and increases inflation.

Inflation

Military spending not only generates unemployment, it is highly inflationary. Over half of the budget controlled by Congress goes for military purchases and salaries. It is the most inflationary form of federal spending. There are two key reasons for this.

First: most military contractors produce on a cost-plus basis. They have no incentive to improve efficiency and cut waste. In fact, the contrary is the case, as contractors get guaranteed profits no matter what the costs incurred. This is the opposite of the free enterprise system.

Second: the federal government must either borrow money or increase the money supply in order to finance skyrocketing military expenditures. Increasing the amount of money in circulation can fuel inflation. Borrowing money decreases the amount of available credit and bids up interest rates. This increases the cost of financing government debt, business investment, and consumer purchases. . . .

The Myth About Military Spending and the Economy

Because of a long held myth, huge military budgets have passed Congress for decades with virtually no comment upon their economic impact. Like many myths, it had its genesis in historical circumstance. Everyone over fifty remembers the Depression. And everyone under fifty has heard about it. The memories of long lines of destitute people waiting at soup kitchens, of men selling apples on the street corners made an indelible impression on the American consciousness.

Then came World War II. Eleven million young men were drafted into the armed forces and war factories were opened all over the country hiring unemployed men and women. Everyone had a job. So the concept that was stamped upon the collective memory of Americans was that the war ended the Depression, and therefore that military spending created jobs.

No one said that the government spending $80 billion in a year in 1941 on *anything* would have ended the Depression. The federal government could have replaced worn out housing, rundown railroads, and decrepit hospitals. Any vast influx of investment and consumption into the system would have terminated

the Depression. But most Americans just observed that when the war began the Depression ended, and therefore assumed military spending must be good for the economy.

Myths die hard. It has taken years of the current economic malaise, the combination of high unemployment, high inflation, and high military spending, to cause people to begin to re-examine their assumptions about the economy and the impact of military spending.

Long Term Growth: Rebuilding the Infrastructure

In order to have the undergirding necessary for sustained industrial growth, our infrastructure must be secure.

Business Week, in an edition devoted to our deteriorating infrastructure, estimated that during the decade of the 1980's, $500 billion would have to be spent on our roads, bridges, public buildings, mass transit systems, and our ports.[8] This is a $2,300 per capita over a 10 year period, only $230 per person per year.

The article said, "The lack of maintenance in recent decades has inflicted serious damage on the roads, bridges, and mass transit systems which is the lifeline of the nation's business. Bad roads and bridges keep 25% of America's communities out of the growth business."

America In Ruins is an important new study by the Council of State Planning Agencies. It reported that,

> In a Bureau of the Census study conducted in the mid 1970's, over 2,000 firms operating in 254 distinct product categories were asked if the availability of certain public works facilities were either (1) criti-cal; (2) significant; or (3) of minimal value in their locational deci-sion. The survey indicated that for virtually all of the 254 product categories studied, the availability of public works facilities was of either critical or significant importance to locational decisions. The availability of public facilities was almost always a more important locational consideration than the availability of local tax incentives or local industrial revenue bond financing. While public works in themselves are never a sufficient condition for economic develop-ment, they are almost always a *necessary* condition.[9]

Conclusions and Recommendations

If $40 billion per year were cut from the Pentagon's budget and allocated to rebuilding America's infrastructure, an impor-tant part of the base for our industrial rebirth would be laid.

8. *Business Week,* "State and Local Governments In Trouble", October 26, 1981, pg. 154.
9. Choate, Pat and Walter, Susan, *America In Ruins*, Council On State Planning Agencies, Washington, 1981, pg. 17.

Although $40 billion sounds like a substantial sum, we were spending at a rate of more than double that in 1965 when public sector construction was 31% of total construction.[10]

Resurfacing and repairing roads, upgrading the railroad system, repairing and building public buildings, rebuilding our bridges which are unsafe, would put 1,200,000 people to work in the construction industry, and 1,440,000 to work in related industries. Steel, cement, fabricated structural metal, lumber, and machinery producing industries as well as architectural and engineering firms would all be immediately and directly affected. Every town, every city in the country would benefit from cleaner water, better transportation, improved public facilities and more business.

10. Choate, op.cit. pg. 9.

"The results of this analysis suggest that additional dollars spent on defense should provide more or less the same employment as additional dollars spent on most nondefense products."

Pentagon Spending Has Little Impact on Jobs

Congressional Budget Office

In February, 1983, the Congressional Budget Office (CBO) released a study on the effect of defense spending on the U.S. economy. The study was conducted at the request of the House Committee on Armed Services in response to the Reagan Administration's proposal of large increases in defense spending. In the following viewpoint, excerpted from the study, the CBO concluded that money spent on defense would create about the same number of jobs as money spent in the civilian sector of the economy. Although the CBO study expressed concern about the long term effects of increased defense spending, it saw few economic risks in the short term.

As you read, consider the following questions:

1. What percent of growth does the CBO predict in defense spending for the years 1984-88?
2. Why does the CBO claim that the short term effects of increased defense spending will not be harmful?
3. How does the CBO suggest that increased defense spending will effect employment and the total number of jobs generated?

Congressional Budget Office, "Defense Spending and the Economy," February 1983. For sale by the Superintendent of Documents, US Government Printing Office, Washington, DC 20402.

The Administration has proposed a succession of large increases in the defense budget for fiscal years 1984 through 1988, following substantial increases over the last several years. The Administration's plan would increase real (inflation adjusted) budget authority for the Department of Defense (DoD) by about 6.9 percent annually for 1984-1988. The 1981-1983 growth averaged about 10 percent annually. The plan emphasizes investment (which includes weapons procurement, military construction, and research and development); after adjustment for inflation, growth in these investment accounts would average 13 percent a year for the entire 1981-1988 period.

When the United States has expanded its arsenals this rapidly in the past, it has also experienced a substantial increase in inflation. The inflation rate rose an average of 3.7 percentage points during the last four major military buildups. Some influential economists have warned that the currently proposed buildup could have similarly deleterious effects on inflation and on productivity.[1]

The choice of appropriate levels of defense spending essentially is a question of priorities, reflecting assessments of the requirements for national security and evaluations of the importance of alternative uses of resources. This choice probably should not be influenced unduly by the effects of defense spending on the economy, since those effects can, in principle, be offset or achieved by other policies. It is, nonetheless, important to be mindful of the economic effects of defense spending, since that knowledge can help in shaping appropriate overall budgetary and monetary policies. This report helps to identify the effects of higher defense spending on inflation, employment, and productivity over the next several years.

Few Economic Risks from Buildup in the Short Term

According to the results of this study, the Administration's proposed defense buildup should neither rekindle inflation nor stunt employment growth over the next few years. This conclusion rests on an assessment of the near-term economic outlook, which is influenced by all aspects of federal budgetary and monetary policies.

Most macroeconomic forecasters currently foresee a sluggish cyclical recovery and continued economic slack that, together, will contribute to a continued gradual slowing of inflation dur-

1. Among them are Henry Kaufman, Wall Street analyst, and Lester Thurow, MIT economist.

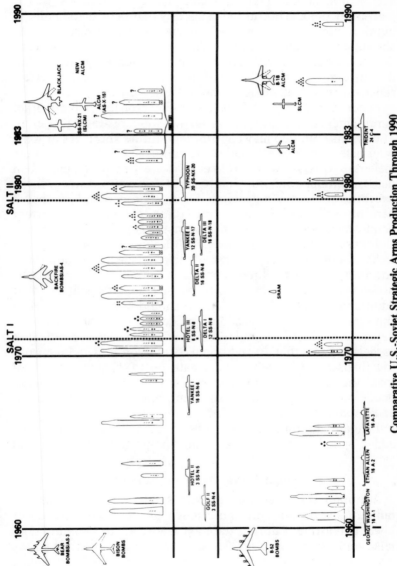

Comparative U.S.-Soviet Strategic Arms Production Through 1990

ing the next few years. The Congressional Budget Office (CBO) forecast, for example, projects that inflation, as measured by the implicit price deflator for gross national product (GNP), will decline from about 6 percent in calendar year 1982 to less than 5 percent in 1985.[2] This outlook suggests that neither the military buildup nor the stimulative posture of overall fiscal policy should pose much risk of rekindling inflation in the near term. On the contrary, the risk that appears most acute is that growing deficits and tight credit conditions will choke off interest-sensitive spending, thereby stalling the recovery. . . .

Labor Availability. An evaluation of probable labor-market developments similarly shows no inflationary wage pressures. The defense buildup may contribute to future shortages of some scientists, engineers, skilled machinists, and tool-and-die makers – categories of workers that are heavily employed in defense production. But, in the next few years, these will be exceptional cases in a generally bleak labor market. Less than 3 percent of the work force falls into these categories, and current employment and unemployment data suggest that labor-market tightness is not pervasive even in these occupations.

Employment Growth. Increased defense spending should not adversely affect overall employment. Contrary to the assertions of some observers, the results of this analysis suggest that additional dollars spent on defense should provide more or less the same employment as additional dollars spent on most non-defense products. Simulations performed on econometric models suggest that an additional $10 billion in defense spending in fiscal year 1983 could create up to 250,000 additional jobs; the same $10 billion spent on purchases of nondefense goods and services could also create almost 250,000 jobs. An additional $10 billion spent entirely on defense purchases might induce an additional 210,000 jobs. The smaller effect from this added spending reflects the greater proportion of highly paid workers in defense industries.

Some Risks Posed by Buildup

Although the foregoing analysis suggests that the defense buildup should not contribute much to increased inflation or lower employment during the next few years, the buildup does raise some economic risks. These risks may grow as time passes and as more is known about the projected economic recovery.

2. Congressional Budget Office, *The Outlook for Economic Recovery* (February 1983).

Defense Budget Trends, Fiscal Years 1950-1988
(In billions of fiscal year 1983 dollars)

Total

Year	Amount	Percent Change
1950	79.4	
1951	224.5	182.9
1952	288.8	28.6
1953	235.0	− 18.6
1954	175.9	− 25.1
1955	149.5	− 15.0
1956	153.6	2.7
1957	163.2	6.3
1958	159.6	− 2.2
1959	170.9	7.1
1960	166.0	− 2.8
1961	165.5	− 0.3
1962	188.5	13.9
1963	191.8	1.7
1964	184.6	− 3.7
1965	177.0	− 4.1
1966	213.1	20.4
1967	232.3	9.0
1968	235.4	1.3
1969	226.5	− 3.8
1970	204.4	− 9.7
1971	183.8	− 10.1
1972	178.9	− 2.7
1973	170.8	− 4.5
1974	165.2	− 3.3
1975	161.5	− 2.3
1976	168.2	4.2
1977	177.2	5.3
1978	174.2	− 1.7
1979	174.4	0.1
1980	178.3	2.3
1981	200.3	12.3
1982	223.8	11.7
1983	239.4	7.0
1984	263.6	10.1
1985	292.6	11.0
1986	308.4	5.4
1987	320.7	4.0
1988	333.5	4.0

Sources: Department of Defense; and CBO projections based on DoD estimates.

Increases in Weapons Prices. Although bottlenecks in major defense-related industries seem unlikely, some may occur in smaller industries specializing in defense production. Such bottlenecks are unlikely to spawn widespread inflation, but they could drive up some weapons prices and increase the costs of the defense buildup.

Growth rates will be high in many specialized defense-intensive industries. After adjustment for inflation, median annual growth from calendar years 1983 to 1985 could be 7.5 percent in the 100 small industries that are most involved in defense production. This is more than double the 3.6 percent growth rate CBO projects for the economy as a whole. For some of these industries, annual real growth rates may run as high as 20 percent over these years. Production is currently depressed in many of these industries, however, and thus these high growth rates might not lead to bottlenecks. . . .

Reductions in Productivity. The defense buildup could also adversely affect increases in productivity in the late 1980s. A strong surge in private demand for capital goods might occur in those years as a result of economic recovery, pent-up demands for business and consumer capital goods, and investment incentives embodied in current tax laws. In such circumstances, the proposed rapid increase in military spending on procurement, construction, and research and development (R&D) could contribute to shortages of capacity to produce capital goods and to shortages of industry engineers and scientists. Nondefense demands might be curtailed disproportionately in the resulting competition for limited resources, resulting in lower private investment and R&D and, hence, lower productivity. The associated imbalances in markets for capital goods and for technically trained personnel could contribute to a slowdown in economic activity that, in itself, could delay private-sector productivity gains. Note that these risks hinge on the possibility that shifts in demand might be unusually sudden or large, rather than on the theory that defense spending invariably retards productivity. The statistical evidence for this latter proposition is ambiguous.

Increased Inflation through Faster Economic Growth. The analysis thus far has assumed that the economy will recover sluggishly, in line with the CBO forecast. The future always holds surprises, however. If the private economy recover more rapidly than currently forecast, then the proposed buildup could increase risks of renewed inflation and of crowding out of private borrowing in financial markets.

The economy might, for example, experience an average cyclical recovery. This would entail real GNP growth of more than 6 percent in 1983 and about 16 percent cumulatively for the 1983-1985 period, compared with the CBO forecast of only 2.1 percent in 1983 and about 11 percent cumulatively from 1983 through 1985. If this more robust recovery occurred, capacity utilization in manufacturing would edge above the 85 percent level associated with full employment by the end of 1985. Capacity utilization in each of the seven major, defense-intensive manufacturing sectors, except steel, would exceed historical averages by a wide margin. The outlook for business investment is particularly important. A surge in investment – which is characteristic of an average cyclical recovery – could overextend the high-technology industries which are already forecast to be operating at rather high rates in 1985.

Serious Risk in Longer Run if Buildup Financed with Deficits. In the longer run, as the economy approaches full employment of resources, deficits caused by the defense buildup and other fiscal policies could pose a serious risk. Risks would derive, in part, from budget initiatives taken over the last two years. The Administration and the Congress have boosted defense spending while reducing tax burdens and curbing growth in nondefense spending. The combination of higher defense spending and lower tax revenues, even after offsetting tax increases in 1982, added more to the deficit than nondefense spending reductions cut from it. As a result, CBO projects that – without further Congressional action – the unified federal deficit will remain around $200 billion through fiscal year 1985 and increase to nearly $270 billion by 1988. Even measured at high-employment levels of income and employment, the deficit is projected to increase from $90 billion in fiscal year 1984 to $130 billion in 1985 and to more than $200 billion in 1988. This suggests that, without changes in current policies, fiscal policy will remain stimulative, with attendant inflationary pressures, as the economy approaches full employment.

The nature of the growing defense budget – with its emphasis on procurement – increases long-run concerns. The Congress, in appropriating money for defense procurement, commits funds years in advance of actual spending. Indeed, one dollar in an average defense procurement contract produces outlays of only about 12 cents in the first year, and outlays from that contract may continue over five years or more. If the Congress commits itself to high levels of defense procurement spending, it could have difficulty moderating fiscal stimulus in the future when the

147

economy approaches full employment of resources.

These observations suggest that some combination of prospective reductions in defense or nondefense spending or increases in taxes are critical to avoid over-stimulating the economy after 1985. Without them, higher inflation would, in time, be likely. If inflation was restrained by monetary rather than fiscal policy, then high interest rates and sluggish economic growth would be probable.

Conclusion

The ultimate decision on procurement and other defense spending principally should depend on considerations of national security and priorities for the use of resources. Current forecasts suggest that the proposed rapid defense buildup need not rekindle inflation in the near term. The buildup could, nonetheless, contribute to tightness in some particular industries that do a great deal of defense work. This could raise risks of cost growth and delivery delays in weapons systems. Moreover, a defense buildup financed by large federal deficits that continue even after the economy recovers could damage economic performance in the longer run.

"It is difficult to find any military justification for this dramatic rush to acquire more weapons."

Military Spending Should Be Reduced

Center for Defense Information

The Center for Defense Information (CDI) describes itself as a non-profit, non-partisan research organization. Claiming to support a strong defense, it opposes excesses and waste in military spending and programs that increase the danger of nuclear war. CDI believes that strong social, economic, and political structures contribute equally to national security and thus are essential to the strength of America. The following viewpoint taken from a 1983 issue of its publication *The Defense Monitor*, concludes that the Reagan Administration's call for increased defense spending is both unnecessary and wasteful.

As you read, consider the following questions:

1. Why does CDI claim it is time to create a Congressional Office of Defense Appraisal?
2. What is the "Phony Crisis" CDI refers to?
3. What does CDI say about comparing U.S. military spending to estimates of Soviet spending?

Center for Defense Information, "The Need for a Level Military Budget," *The Defense Monitor*, Vol. XII, No. 2. © 1983 by Center for Defense Information.

President Ronald Reagan and Secretary of Defense Caspar Weinberger assert that their proposed $280.5 Billion military budget for fiscal 1984 cannot be reduced. With no supporting evidence they further assert this figure is the absolute minimum required for the defense of the United States. Weinberger has pitted his modest experience in military matters against the combined expertise of the Congress by threatening that if legislators reduce the requested military budget, "the Congress would be, I think, endangering the security of this country."

The fact of the matter, however, is that nobody knows for certain precisely how large the military budget should be. As in other controversial areas – the economy, inflation, and energy – there is no clear way to meaure appropriateness. General George Brown, former Chairman of the Joint Chiefs of Staff said, "How much is adequate is largely subjective because it depends upon uncountable factors." Such candor is all too rare.

As a nation, we cannot continually increase military spending in real terms year after year. Sooner or later it will be necessary to level off this spending and the longer we delay the more difficult it will be. Military spending has already increased much more than is necessary. . . .

In the nuclear era, there is little relationship between amounts of military spending and an adequate national defense posture. Military budgets are frequently framed by many factors that have little to do with military capabilities. Military budgets have recently been used by politicians as vehicles for sending "messages" and "symbols" of will and intention. As Mr. Weinberger said at the start of the Reagan Administration, this is "a time when we should be seen as getting stronger"; ergo, we should spend more money.

In a simplistic fashion Mr. Weinberger equates increased military spending with increased strength. By his formula "real growth" in military expenditures demonstrates real growth in military capability.

In creating a politically charged climate of alarm by alleging U.S. military weaknesses, Mr. Reagan and Mr. Weinberger have stampeded the Congress and the American people into allocating vast sums of money for the military. Our military spending rose more than 68% between 1980 and 1983 – an unprecedented rise during peacetime in American history. . . .

Money Should Be Spent Prudently

It is obvious we must spend whatever is necessary for the defense of the U.S. but it must be prudently spent. Military

spending should be measured against a few extremely important criteria. We should buy weapons which are clearly needed and we should buy weapons which have a high probability of working effectively if called upon in war. We should *not* buy weapons which are of only marginal effectiveness. We should *not* buy weapons which we do not know where or how they are to be used. What we should do is carefully, even cautiously, add new weapons so as to have those weapons which we need, which will work when we need them, and equally important, which will not be outmoded in the near future.

Beetle Bailey, reprinted with permission from King Features Syndicate Division.

Our long-term national security requires that we maintain a rough equilibrium in our ability to pay for weapons and our estimated military requirements. If we rush headlong into a vast military expansion, as Mr. Weinberger is urging, the drain on our economy will unbalance our national security structure.

The process by which weapons are acquired in peacetime should be carefully programmed to avoid highs and lows in purchases. If we buy too many in the short run, we almost certainly will have an obsolete force in a few years. Prudence in weapons acquisition suggests that the lowest possible expenditures be maintained concurrent with needs. In this way there will be room for expansion in a crisis, and at the same time assure the availability of funds for maintenance of a modern military force in future years.

The time has come to create a Congressional Office of Defense Appraisal (CODA) to deal with such matters. Today there is no place in the Congress where a larger view of military affairs is considered, where all factors relevant to national security, both military and non-military, are integrated. A Congressional Office of Defense Appraisal could provide a centralized, coherent integration of U.S. military strategy, available resources, and military spending. Today's piecemeal approach allows the

national security bureaucracy and military spending to grow rapidly with no attempt made to insure that strategy, forces, and other national objectives are mutually supportive. Such an office would facilitate Congress' legal requirement to provide for raising and supporting the military forces of the United States in consonance with overall national security.

The Phony Crisis

There is a frantic tone to the Secretary of Defense's statements in his report to the Congress for fiscal year 1984. He conveys a sense of immediate, impending danger of a Soviet attack on the U.S. or our interests throughout the world. As he sees it, "Soviet power threatens us directly and poses obstacles to the successful conduct of our foreign policy. . . . The deterrent strength of the Atlantic Alliance is increasingly threatened offering opportunities for Soviet coercion in the event of crisis." This excessive fear of potential Soviet actions against the United States is to be countered by ever more rapid increases in military spending for new nuclear and conventional weapons. It is difficult to find any military justification for this dramatic rush to acquire more weapons.

Many "facts" are included in the posture statement to support this fear – facts that indicate increasing Soviet force levels and military spending. However, "inconvenient facts" which were omitted from the posture statement provide a more balanced perspective. For instance, the United States has always had more nuclear weapons than the Soviet Union, and the NATO nations spend more on defense and have more personnel in uniform than the forces of the Warsaw Pact. Top U.S. military leaders and President Reagan have all said they would not trade our military forces for those of the Soviets.

The overall situation has not suddenly become dangerous. However, if the Administration is convinced that we are in immediate danger, they should call for mobilizing the national guard and the reserves and put the economy on an emergency status. If our strategic forces are in such bad shape, why has Mr. Weinberger decommissioned five Polaris submarines before the end of their useful lives and removed the missile launching capability of five others? Why has he ordered the retirement of 52 of our largest land-based ICBMs and the B-52D bomber force? The answer is obvious: we have an adequate, strong, and effective military force. In the meantime Mr. Weinberger continues using scare tactics to panic the American people and the Congress into buying weapons without adequate justification.

The Death Watch

I recently read a pathetic story which may contain a moral for us all.

There's a pleasant (if somewhat shabby) neighborhood on the West Side of Cleveland which has a large percentage of elderly residents. These folks are mostly pretty sociable, but there is one neighbor – a Mr. Wesley – who was something of a loner. So the other people on his street didn't think it too unusual when they didn't see him for weeks at a stretch.

But last week, when it was noticed that his newspaper and his mail were stacking up on the porch, and when he repeatedly failed to respond to the doorbell and the phone, the authorities decided to break in and see what was going on.

They found poor Mr. Wesley dead in bed, surrounded by rifles, pistols and guns of every description. Boxes of bullets and cartridges were stacked on the floor. There was a knife in Mr. Wesley's hand, and – believe it or not – a harpoon leaning up against the refrigerator, which was empty.

Mr. Wesley had died of starvation.

There were other contributing factors: an untreated respiratory infection, for instance. But the outstanding fact is that Mr. Wesley had spent all his money – his Social Security check, his pension, everything – on guns. He was afraid of burglars (with good reason, of course). But his fear was an obsession. And in the end, it killed him.

So it is with us. Every couple of years, the military madness overtakes us. We spend and spend. We postpone plans indefinitely for sewage treatment plants along the Great Lakes, while we manufacture F-111's. We let our own cities, struggle, stink, and sink while we supply expensive weaponry to all sides in the Mideast. We stack "boxes of bullets and cartridges" all over the continent, while we exhaust precious resources of soil, water and air.

But the pity is that our expensive obsession will not save us from our real enemies, any more than Mr. Wesley's harpoon could save him.

Now is the time to study our options.

If we don't, we may end up like poor Mr. Wesley; armed to the teeth, and waiting for death.

Juli Loesch, "The Death Watch." Reprinted with permission of *Erie Christian Witness*, published by Pax Center, Erie, PA 16503.

Too Much Too Fast

The National Defense budget was $145.8 Billion in 1980. The request for 1984 has almost doubled to $280.5 Billion. Mr. Weinberger says he wants $432 Billion in 1988. This projected rise of nearly 300% in eight years will set new peacetime records. This

year's request in real terms is about 13% higher than that which was spent during the height of the Vietnam war. The increases are largely associated with buying more war-fighting weapons. Spending for new weapons, military construction, and research and development has dramatically escalated from 36% of the total military budget in 1980 to a proposed 47% in 1984. By 1988 over half of the military budget will be used to pay for new weapons. If this trend continues readiness for combat will suffer.

Because of the vast array of new, complex, expensive weapons that are to be built in a very short period, it is almost certain that there will be increased waste of materials and reduced efficiency in their production. The poor record of the Defense Department in controlling escalating weapon costs will only worsen. The Congressional Budget Office reported that of 60 major weapons being built in 1983, 35 weapons showed significant real growth in unit costs. In addition, these large weapon construction programs will have a detrimental effect on the future of the economy because rapidly increased spending cannot be adequately controlled by the Pentagon. Murray Weidenbaum, former Chairman of the Council of Economic Advisors, emphasized this point when he said, "I worry that we might be going faster, on a bigger scale than our economy can sustain." Former Secretary of Defense Melvin Laird, a proponent of a strong defense posture, cautioned that, "The worst thing that can happen is to go on a defense spending binge that will create economic havoc at home and confusion abroad and that cannot be dealt with wisely by the Pentagon." . . .

U.S. Treasury Is Broke

The 1984 federal deficit is expected to be nearly $200 Billion. If standby taxes are not enacted the deficit in 1988 may be about $300 Billion. Even with these new taxes, the deficit in 1988 would still be almost $120 Billion. Military spending has contributed significantly to the 1984 deficit; the increase in military spending from 1980 to 1984 will be $135 Billion. Every knowledgeable person, every economic survey made recognizes the deleterious effect of ever-increasing military spending. A recent study conducted by the House Committee on the Budget joined the rising chorus when it noted that, "the rapid rise in the structural deficit results from excessive tax reductions, rapid growth in military spending, and the much higher interest on the larger debt issued to finance these policies." However, like the weather, everyone talks about the adverse effect of increas-

ing military spending but no one does anything about it.

Cost Growth and Waste

Despite efforts by Secretary Weinberger to improve the Pentagon's record, wasteful spending continues. Most vexing is the growth in weapon costs that is caused by Pentagon practices such as optimistically lowering inflation estimates, intentionally submitting low cost estimates, making significant changes in specifications, and failing to insist on adequate competition.

The problem of cost escalation is exacerbated by the increased pace of weapons purchases because industry is slow to adjust to the increased demand. For instance, though real inflation in the country was only about 5% in 1982, inflation in the defense industry was 14%.

When the Defense Department presents a proposal to Congress for a new weapons system, the proposal almost always includes a desired number of weapons in the total buy. Many times, because costs were purposely estimated too low, the number of weapons ultimately acquired is cut dramatically. We end up spending more and getting less, an extremely discouraging phenomenon that reinforces the need for a thorough overhaul of the manner in which weapons are purchased.

Soviet Superiority?

Secretary Weinberger persistently charges, "Failure of the United States and its key allies to keep pace with the Soviet bloc (primarily Soviet) military buildup has not only enabled the Soviet Union to turn to a more offensive force posture, but has also resulted in a shift in the military balance." Harping on the same theme last November, President Reagan stated, "Today in virtually every measure of military power, the Soviet Union enjoys a decided advantage."

Ever since he took office the President has based his military program on the CIA's estimate of what the Soviets spend for their military. This makes little sense for several reasons. Comparison of U.S. military expenditures with estimates of Soviet expenditures is an inexact art based on sketchy information, assumptions, and difficulties in translating ruble costs into dollar values. Such estimates should never be used to make signficant decisions on how much the United States should spend for its military forces, especially since it has been recently revealed that the CIA has for years been overestimating the annual rate of growth of Soviet military spending by at least 50%. In recent years Soviet military spending has increased a modest 2% each year, according to current U.S. calculations. By

comparison, since 1976 U.S. military spending has increased in real terms at an annual rate of more than 5%. . . .

Conclusions

• The growth of military spending can be reduced from its present high level without endangering the security of the coun-˙ try. National security has many more factors than military might, most of which would benefit from this reduction.

• The way to reduce spending is to eliminate those weapon systems that are unnecessary and to reduce the other categories of spending that are bloated because of the presence of these unnecessary weapons.

• A Congressional Office of Defense Appraisal should be established immediately to integrate all aspects of military spending with other national priorities.

> *"We really have no viable alternative to the establishment of a defense program geared to curtail and to deter the potential Soviet threat."*

Defense Spending Is Justified

Samuel S. Stratton

Samuel Stratton is a democratic congressman from New York state. He is a member of the House Armed Services Committee and chairman of its Procurement and Military Nuclear System Subcommittee. In the following viewpoint, written for *USA Today* magazine, Congressman Stratton claims the criticism of the Reagan buildup is not well-founded. He argues that weapons cost more today because the threat is greater.

As you read, consider the following questions:

1. Why does Congressman Stratton think the U.S. is more vulnerable now than it was before the Cuban missile crisis of 1962?
2. What evidence does the Congressman present to prove that "the Soviet war machine" is more powerful than U.S. forces?
3. Although he feels they are necessary, what explanation does the author give for the high cost of today's weapons?

Samuel S. Stratton, "National Affairs: Is the High Cost of Defense Spending Justified? YES." Reprinted from USA TODAY, September 1982. © Copyright 1982 by Society for the Advancement of Education.

Throughout the course of our history, national defense has been a controversial issue. Americans understandably dislike and detest war, and as a consequence the discussions on the annual defense budget are apt to be heated in Congress. Our dislike for war is evidenced by the fact that we have never been really prepared to enter the wars that obviously had to be fought to preserve our freedom and security.

The two major factions that engage in the annual Congressional defense debates are the pro-defense advocates, who believe we are not spending enough for defense, and the anti-defense contingent, who seem to oppose every single defense program or project.

I find myself among the former, not because I subscribe to everything the Pentagon advocates – quite the contrary – but because as long as there are ideological, political, religious, and cultural differences among nations, and as long as there is a desire on the part of some government leaders to exploit the people and the territorial boundaries of others, there will be a need for an effective national defense. That truth is, of course, even more valid in the case of the free world's only superpower.

However, the question raised in this confrontation goes beyond that particular point. In today's inflated world, the cost of weapons systems has indeed escalated. Is that high cost justified? Or, put another way, can we really afford *not* to pay for the weapons we must have to deter our potential adversaries?

Peace Through Strength

National defense is not only a complex, but also an emotional, issue. It encompasses both logic and paradox. It was George Washington who first expressed the theory of "peace through strength," which implies that a nation must build in advance the tools of war if it is to avoid the outbreak of war and hence maintain the peace. In contemporary language, this is the theory of "deterrence" – the basis for our strategic triad of intercontinental ballistic missiles (ICBM's), submarine-launched ballistic missiles (SLBM's), and manned penetrating bombers. Deterrence leads in turn to what is the most dramatic paradox of all – that our most devastating nuclear weapons are most successful when they are *not* being used. Thus, our aging Minuteman ICBM's and Poseidon SLBM's and our obsolete B-52 nuclear bomber force – though they have never been used – have successfully saved us, for over 37 years, from a nuclear World War III. One can only conjecture what the current state of world affairs would be if it

were the Soviets who had held the strategic nuclear monopoly.

The structuring of an adequate defense program depends on a number of complicated variables, including the threat to our society, world tensions, the state of our economy, social needs and requirements, the availability of critical resources that affect our economic lifeline, and a host of other factors. Moreover, there are different opinions as to just what constitutes a "threat" to our society. As a result, the balance between military and

---

The Liberal Defense Myth

The defense platform of Congressional liberals has emphasized reducing President Reagan's defense budget to levels which mirror the inadequate budget proposals of the Carter Administration. This, on the belief, that "Ronald Reagan's compulsive spending on defense would make us weaker, not stronger."

To that end, many in Congress have sought to take away funds from defense in order to resume rapid increases in social spending at the cost of reduced military capability.

The danger lies not in increasing social spending *per se*, but rather in the destructive notion that somehow an adequate defense may be rebuilt and then maintained with less funds than are actually required. The perpetuation of such a myth is the greatest deception of all. For it supposes to soothe the legitimate concerns of Americans who see an ever-growing Soviet arsenal supporting adventurism abroad as a precurser to armed conflict. Instead, it merely transmits the inevitable responsibility to provide for the collective defense to a later generation at an increased cost in both funds and international instability.

"The Liberal Defense Agenda," *National Security Record*, May 1983 by The Heritage Foundation.

---

social spending becomes, as it has in recent Congressional budget debates, more of an emotional and political issue than a strictly technical one. The emotional aspect gives rise to all kinds of catchy cliches and buzzwords that are used in the defense debate. A Congressman who supports a strong defense, for example, is certain to be dubbed a "Pentagon lackey" or a "hawk," while a consistent opponent of defense will be branded a "dove." If one is part of a company that develops military weapons systems, then he automatically becomes part of the so-called "military industrial complex" and as such finds himself accused by defense critics of profiteering under the guise of national security.

Let me focus, however, on the one factor that should have the overwhelming influence on defense needs – the potential enemy

threat. Remember 1960? The U.S. was the most powerful nation in the world in those days. Our future was secure, and our worldwide interests were not seen as seriously challenged. We héld a virtual monopoly on nuclear power and weaponry, but never dreamed of using it to dominate the rest of the world. In 1962, when the Soviet Union tried to sneak nuclear missiles into Cuba, we had both the national will and the direct means to end that threat without firing a single shot. To most Americans, that was a high-water mark in our military and foreign policy. Yet, the fact is that that diplomatic and military "victory," won by the courage and skill of Pres. Kennedy, had far-reaching consequences which few of us in Congress recognized at the time.

At a subsequent meeting in Connecticut with former Army Secretary and High Commissioner to Germany John J. McCloy, representing Pres. Kennedy, V.V. Kuznetsov (now First Deputy Chairman of the Presidium of the Supreme Soviet), then representing Chairman Khrushchev, made this assertion to McCloy:

> All right, we will remove the IL-28's from Cuba as agreed between us, and we will keep this agreement as we intend to keep our assurances about removal of the missiles. But I want you to understand, Mr. McCloy, that this is the last time the U.S. will be able to impose such conditions on the Soviet Union.

From that date on, as we later learned, the Soviets left no doubt that they intended to establish military superiority over the U.S. and "to surpass the U.S. in virtually every area of military technology and capability."

During the decade of the 1970's, while we were still wobbling from the effects of the "Vietnam syndrome," the Soviets outspent us by over $400,000,000,000 in military investment (research and development, procurement, construction, etc.). The difference between Soviet and U.S. expenditures would itself have funded the development and procurement of 244 B-1 aircraft, 4,600 MX shelters with a full complement of 200 missiles, eight Trident submarines with about 200 Trident missiles, 7,000 M-1 tanks and 3,000 armored personnel carriers to support the tanks, and all the F-14, F-15, F-16, F-18, and A-10 aircraft required to modernize completely our tactical air forces.

The Soviet War Machine

Indeed, since the Soviet humiliation in the Cuban missile crisis, no military area – strategic, chemical, conventional, land, sea, or air – has been overlooked by the Russians in constructing the most massive war machine ever built in the history of man-

kind, not even excepting Adolf Hitler's. Today, the Soviets possess the world's largest ballistic missile submarine, the Typhoon; the world's largest cruise missile-carrying submarine, the Oscar; and the world's fastest attack submarine, the 40-knot-and-above Alpha. In tank forces, the Russians outnumber us seven-to-one, and in artillery, six-to-one. They have at least three times as many tactical aircraft as we do, 50 times the number of trained and active chemical warfare personnel, and three times as many attack submarines. In terms of production capacity, the Soviets' annual production of tanks between 1971 and 1975 was 3,030, compared to our 415. During that same period, they built three times as many submarines, three times as many tactical aircraft, and from two to 11 times more other military equipment than the U.S. Currently, the Soviets have another 50 major weapons systems in various stages of research and development, test and evaluation, and production.

These static indicators – the number of tanks, aircraft, ships, etc. – convey a frightening, but, alas, highly accurate, picture of the Soviet war-fighting capability. How much of a threat this capability represents to the free world may be – and indeed is – heatedly argued. However, in my judgment, such a vast military inventory far surpasses what is required for the defense of the Soviet homeland. Whatever may be the true Soviet intentions, and while communism is admittedly no longer monolithic, there is no hard evidence to suggest that the Soviet leaders have deviated in any degree from the principal Marxist-Leninist objective – the destruction of capitalism and ultimate communist world domination. In the concluding words of the Communist Internationale, "The International Soviet shall be the human race."

In these circumstances, our leaders in the White House, the Pentagon, and the Congress would be criminally derelict if we were not to give serious consideration to the possibility that this massive, military juggernaut might some day be vectored against us. If it makes sense, as I believe, to subscribe to this possibility, then we must, at our peril, move swiftly to counter the possible threat.

Some people contend that the massive Soviet military investment will bankrupt their economy, but this process has been going on for over 10 years and I have seen no data to suggest that the Soviet system is on the verge of collapse. Moreover, considering how very little we really know about the Soviet economy or the intentions of the Soviet leadership, it strikes me as foolish in the extreme to structure a U.S. national security

program based on the expectation of the failure of the Soviet economy within the foreseeable future. So, we really have no viable alternative to the establishment of a defense program geared to curtail and to deter the potential Soviet threat. To do otherwise could invite national suicide.

Once we have made this decision, it becomes necessary to determine just how much of our national resources we are willing to devote to the task. This is the most critical question that Congress and the Executive Branch have to wrestle with year after year.

Not everyone, as we know, is likely to accept the estimate of the intelligence community, which I have outlined above (in unclassified form) on the size of that threat. It has been customary of those who – for one reason or another – always oppose defense expenditures every spring to charge that, during the budget-making process, overvigilant Navy commanders always seem to sight innumerable surfaced Soviet submarines which somehow never seem to put their superstructures above water after the budget process has been completed.

Even if we were to declassify some of the most sensitive intelligence reports for these doubting Congressmen, many will still say it is a big trick! Others trot out the curious notion that, regardless of the enormous, unprecedented size of the Soviet threat, there exists some "minimum deterrent" which will, all by itself, forestall any possible Soviet attack. This is the substance of a remark once made by Henry Kissinger (but, I understand, subsequently retracted by him) in which he complained to Secretary of Defense James Schlesinger that, beyond a certain point in nuclear weaponry, the word superiority had no meaning! How often are we challenged with the glib assertion that "We can already destroy the Soviet Union 15 times over; why do we have to spend money to destroy it 16 times over?"

Some people have even tried to imply that, as long as we have one or two Polaris or Poseidon submarines, we can bring the whole Soviet nuclear war machine to a screeching halt! These armchair strategists forget that even in the heyday of the American Wild West the desperadoes all carried *six*shooters.
. . .

The Growing Cost of Weapons

Undoubtedly, the costs of responding to the Soviet threat have been, and will remain, high. These costs have been signaled out by defense critics for major attack. Yet, to a very large extent, these criticisms are not well-founded. There are, alas, reasonable

'FOUL!'

Don Hesse, *St. Louis Globe/Democrat*. Reprinted with permission.

explanations for why weapons cost as much as they do today, just as nearly everything else does.

Weapons cost more because the threat requires that they do more. It is interesting, for example, to note that fighter and interceptor aircraft today fly faster straight up than World War II aircraft could fly straight down. The Soviet Foxbat interceptor set the world's time to climb record in 1976, climbing to 110,000 feet in slightly under three minutes and 10 seconds.

Some defense critics suggest our weapons are too sophisticated and that we ought to build simpler, smaller, and less expensive equipment. This has been the general theme of the military systems analysts – that august body of strategists who have been said to know the cost of everything and the military value of very little. I strongly disagree with this approach, because I am unwilling to send our young men into combat with equipment produced solely on the basis of a low bid and which is inferior to the equipment of our adversary. In time of war, cheaper is never better. Over the years, we have become so cost conscious in building combat ships that we have reduced them in size, in combat capability, and in survivability, as the British learned to their sorrow in the South Atlantic. To make our ships lighter, we have used aluminum rather than steel in the superstructure. Aluminum has one undesirable characteristic – it burns when struck by an incoming projectile or missile, as we also saw in the South Atlantic. Today's ships are far more vulnerable to Exocet, Harpoon, or Soviet SS-N-2 cruise missiles than the World War II destroyers that we have retired, as we also saw in the Falkland Islands.

So, if we need our weapons to do more, if we want to enhance the survivability of our forces on the battlefield, or at sea, then the weapons systems to do those jobs are certain to cost more.

A second reason for the high cost of weapons systems is the inefficient means by which we procure them. In the automobile industry, General Motors, Chrysler, Ford, or American Motors establish production lines and production quotas. Similarly, a defense contractor must assemble a production line, optimized to build a certain number of items a month. If the line is underutilized, we pay for excess capacity and the unit cost of the article goes up. Because of executive or legislative budget constraints, it is not always possible to procure every weapons system at the optimum production rate. In the defense industry, however, it is important to note that we have been unable to procure even a *single* major weapon system at the minimum economic rate. This is best illustrated by reviewing the history of the Air Force F-15 and the Navy F-18 tactical fighter aircraft programs.

In 1975, the Office of Management and Budget (OMB) reduced the planned Air Force buy for fiscal year 1976 from 144 to 72 F-15 aircraft. The contractor's plant ws facilitized so that a production rate of less than nine aircraft per month would result in the underutilization of the assembly-line. This OMB reduction

added $500,000,000 to the total cost of the F-15 program through stretchout and the concomitant increase in inflation, a senseless burden for the American taxpayer.

The Carter Administration proposed and the Reagan Administration sustained a recommendation to defer the procurement of 440 Navy F-18 tactical aircraft into the outyears. The deferral has already increased the cost of the F-18 program by over $1,000,-000,000. . . .

The Inflation Factor

Finally, like everything else, defense costs far more today than it did a decade ago. Inflation has been as unkind to defense as it has been to consumer goods. The Economic Indicators of March, 1982, published by the Council of Economic Advisors depict graphically the 10-year profile of the U.S. economy. Between 1972 and 1982, both consumer prices and the producer's price index for all finished goods increased by over 100%. In spite of the doubling of prices, we must still buy essential commodities and goods, but in the midst of economic hardship. Why, then, is it so difficult to accept the fact that weapons systems – just as automobiles, housing, travel, etc. – have increased substantially in cost?

I would conjecture that defense expenditures are difficult to accept because, as I said at the outset, Americans basically detest the idea of war. We should, and we do, know better, but military preparedness is all too often confused as a cause of war. Americans have become fatigued with the need to maintain a strong, national defense year after year – a large force of missiles, ships, tanks, aircraft, etc. – and to keep these weapons all ready and modern. Their fatigue is further exacerbated by pressing domestic and social problems, and, as often happens, they seek a scapegoat; they criticize the defense establishment instead of the real culprit – the Soviet Union and its unprecedented, massive military build-up. . . .

Conclusion

In today's climate, military expenditures are once again coming under serious fire in the Congress. There is no question in my mind, however, that the military capability and objectives of the Soviet Union justify whatever defense expenditures are needed to deter them.

Of course, there is room for improvement in defense acquisition, but, while I am concerned about the cost of weapons, I am no less appalled by the high cost of "economy" import cars, housing, travel, utilities, and telephone calls. I wish we did not

have to spend one single dime on national defense, but there is little to be gained by providing all Americans with the good life unless we are prepared to secure that free way of life against any challenge to it.

I believe it makes good sense to heed the warning of Milovan Djilas, a former leader of Yugoslavia's communist government, when he said, "All armaments in a sense represent waste to mankind. But the cost is only a fraction of what the West will pay if the Soviet forces are led to believe that they will not be stopped."

Recognizing Ethnocentrism

Ethnocentrism is the attitude or tendency of people to view their race, religion, culture, group, or nation as superior to others, and to judge others on that basis. An American, whose custom is to eat with a fork or spoon, would be making an ethnocentric statement when saying, "The Chinese custom of eating with chopsticks is stupid."

Ethnocentrism has promoted much misunderstanding and conflict. It emphasizes cultural and religious differences and the notion that one's national institutions or group's customs are superior.

Ethnocentrism limits people's ability to be objective and to learn from others. Education in the truest sense stresses the similarities of the human condition throughout the world and the basic equality and dignity of all people.

The following statements are taken from chapter three of this book. Consider each statement carefully. *Mark E for any statement you think is ethnocentric. Mark N for any statement you think is not ethnocentric. Mark U if you are undecided about any statement.*

If you are doing this activity as the member of a class or group, compare your answers with those of other class or group members. Be able to defend your answers. You may discover that others will come to different conclusions than you. Listening to the reasons others present for their answers may give you valuable insights in recognizing ethnocentric statements.

If you are reading this book alone, ask others if they agree with your answers. You too will find this interaction very valuable.

E = *ethnocentric*
N = *not ethnocentric*
U = *undecided*

1. The US is the world leader in international arms sales.

2. The surest key to peace is for America to have military superiority over all other nations in the world.

3. The responsibility to defend Western civilization has fallen to the United States because of our superior wealth, resources, and technological skills.

4. The Soviet Union today is the most powerfully armed expansionist nation in the world.

5. I'd rather be slaughtered than slaughter – I believe that that is our moral obligation.

6. The United States represents hope, freedom, security, and peace; the Soviet Union stands for fear, tyranny, aggression, and war.

7. Soviet military forces control Poland.

8. America's greatest strength in this global contest is America itself – our people, our land, our system, our culture, our tradition, our reputation.

9. We know that nuclear weapons cannot threaten the sovereignty of God or of God's creation, but that nuclear weapons in the hands of the Soviets can threaten the survival of Christian civilization.

10. If we want to combat the "red menace," bombs won't do it. Offering a better ideology than Marx might. We need to get even closer to the bible than Marx did.

11. The entire war-fighting posture of the Soviet General Staff rests on the mass use of nuclear missiles.

12. From the earliest days of our republic we have loved peace and been suspicious of things military.

13. Both sides have overabundant nuclear arsenals, sufficiently protected from attack, to obliterate the other after absorbing a first strike, if necesary.

14. Our nation bears no guilt whatsoever for threatening the peace of the world.

Is a Draft Necessary?

"The draft is a fair and equitable means by which free people distribute the burden to remain free."

The Draft Is Necessary

Walter W. Benjamin

Dr. Walter W. Benjamin is chairperson of the Religion Department at Hamline University in St. Paul, Minnesota. In the viewpoint below, he claims that America needs the draft because it would act as a nuclear deterrent. He maintains that only if America has sufficient manpower in uniform can it stop threatening to retaliate against massive conventional aggression with a nuclear counterattack. He also supports the idea that a draft would improve the quality of the U.S. military forces.

As you read, consider the following questions:

1. The author presents six arguments supporting a draft. Which one do you think is most persuasive?
2. Why does the author think the draft would act as a nuclear deterrent?

Walter W. Benjamin, "The Necessity of the Draft." Copyright 1983 Christian Century. Reprinted by permission from the October 13, 1982 issue of *Christian Century*.

It is increasingly apparent that the all-volunteer military is a disaster: it is expensive, inequitable, mercenary, ineffective as a fighting force, and of low morale. It is essential to replace it quickly with as fair a draft as we can devise. . . .

Let me make six points that are crucial to the discussion.

1. *In a democracy equal rights imply equal obligations.* The all-volunteer force offends a fundamental principle upon which our nation was founded: that benefits and burdens should be distributed as equitably as possible. During the Civil War an affluent WASP northerner could pay $60 to have an immigrant Irishman sub for him in the draft. During the Vietnam war university student exemptions and high grade point averages allowed economic and intellectual elites to continue life as usual while their blue-collar brothers died in Asian jungles. Psychologists now believe that much campus destruction and hell-raising during the '60s was the result of repressed anger in students who knew they were unfairly privileged.

In his Vietnam classic *A Rumor of War*, Philip Caputo writes:

> Most soldiers came from the ragged fringes of the Great American Dream, from city slums and dirt farms and Appalachian mining towns. With depressing frequency, the words, *2 years school* appeared in the square labeled *Education* in their service record books, and, under *Father's Address*, a number had written, *Unknown*. They were volunteers, but I wondered for how many enlisting had been truly voluntary . . . they had no hope of getting student deferments, like the upper-middle-class boys who would revile them as killers. Some had the Hobson's choice between service or jail. Others were driven by economic and psychological pressures.

Racial demographics make very clear the mercenary nature of the "volunteer" military. A recent Brookings Institute study reveals that 33 per cent of the army and 22 per cent of the Marine Corps is black. If present trends continue, the army will be 42 per cent black by the late 1980s. While recent high levels of unemployment may drive more whites into the military and slow this trend, there is something fundamentally wrong with a society that allows its underclass to escape the unemployment-welfare-nobodiness status only via the route of potential self-sacrifice for the national honor. We may soon have a military whose members are primarily drawn from various minority groups, a black and brown army defending a mainly white nation.

Military service in a democracy is a citizen's obligation, not because it may demand the giving up of one's life, but because arms protect the state that is responsible for the giving and pro-

tecting of human rights. Such rights are not automatic, like the sunrise, gravity and winter snow. If duty is not connected to liberty, rights are taken for granted. Many liberals have 20/20 vision in seeing the injustice of reducing social programs for the poor. Some are ethically myopic in not seeing the injustice of the mercenary nature of our military – of using the marginalized members of our society to enable the bourgeoisie and their children to pursue privatist concerns.

2. *The draft militates against caste, both military and social.* Military service is a partial solvent to caste, whether geographic, racial, social or educational. While the military of necessity is based on a chain of command, the draft forces comradeship among those who would not normally associate with one

MILESTONE

DRAFT AGE YOUTH

THE
FREEDOM
YOU ENJOY
IS
NEVER PAID
FOR
IN FULL

IT'S
A PERMANENT
TIME PAYMENT
PLAN

Don Hesse, *St. Louis Globe/Democrat.* Reprinted with permission.

another – who, indeed, might otherwise not even be aware of each other's existence. Black, brown, white and yellow are compelled to form platoons and companies. Ivy League graduates must associate with those who went to Mediocre U., rural "rubes" with city "slickers," suburbanites with those from the inner city. Military service in Israel, for example, has aided the forces of homogenization in nation building by bringing Ashkenazic and Sephardic Jews together. The former, of European culture and long dominant in Israeli society, are forced to work with their social inferiors, the Middle Eastern Jews, in the army.

At a time when school busing is waning and social-caste formation is increasing, the draft would assure that members of each generation would have at least one experience lifting them out of their region, background and class. Because of this common experience, we would be bound together, aware of what each of us has to offer, and more likely to endure as a national community in the future.

Moreover, those who fear the growth of military elitism should realize that a continual circulation of young men through the armed forces is a democracy's best antidote to Prussianism or a coup d'etat. From the time of Demosthenes to World War II, democracies have found that citizen armies are the best antidote to "Seven Days in May" scenarios. . . .

3. *The draft acts as a nuclear deterrent.* Kingman Brewster, former president of Yale, affirms that if he were to put a peace bumper sticker on his car, it would read, "I'd Rather Be Drafted Than Be Nuked!" A realistic antinuclear position, he holds, requires some form of draft, for without conscription we might be forced to use nuclear weapons to avoid having Europe overrun by massive, conventional Soviet forces. We presently run that risk because NATO forces are both quantitatively and qualitatively inferior to Warsaw pact forces.

When President Carter tried to persuade our European allies to be more resolute in dealing with Soviet aggression, West German chancellor Helmut Schmidt responded, "There's a difference between a country that has a military service obligation through which its young men are required to participate in the defense of their country and a country that has abolished the draft." Both our friends and foes view the draft as the litmus test of a nation's willingness to fight for its vital interests.

Nations tend to violate the moral principle of proportionality (e.g., armed response should be commensurate with the violence of the attack) if they are deficient in the full range of military

options. Who was it who said, "If the only tool you have is a hammer, everything you see looks like a nail"? The draft would no more increase the potential for war than adding more police would increase a city's crime rate. Only if we have both sufficient manpower in uniform and ready reserves can we stop threatening to retaliate to massive conventional aggression with a nuclear counterattack. It is terrifying to me that we cannot give up the "nuclear option" threat because we are so weak in conventional forces.

4. *The draft contributes to the shaping of character.* Because the Vietnam tragedy is still so vivid in our national consciousness, it is hard for many to see any personal benefit growing out of military service. It has been 20 years since we thrilled to hear, "Ask not what your country can do for you; ask what you can do for your country." We may be losing our sense of participation in the great American experiment. Until Vietnam, few questioned the nation's right to demand a year or two of one's life as the price of citizenship. Now a quasi-isolationist, "never again" funk hangs heavy over the land.

An antidraft stance, however, does not necessarily mean loyalty to altruistic virtues. Our society is surfeited with narcissism, privatism, materialism and hedonism. . . .

American youth who are worried about adolescence, acne, sexuality, space wars and a home in a good corporation are a rather sad lot when compared to Israeli sabras, Arab and Afghan freedom fighters, and Polish Solidarity workers who are simply worried about their country and their lives.

I do not mythologize either war or the military, but there is something to be said for the dose of realism that comes with military service. So much of existence is banal, passionless and noncommunal. Maybe life is not meant to be lived for having "fun" and being obsessed with our own skin; maybe we mature by going through the dark tunnel of danger and mortality in camaraderie and shared purpose and sacrifice. Perhaps there is something missing in a generation of hypersensitive, "untainted" men; something real and deeper than can be dismissed with the facile indictment of "macho." . . .

Liberal societies are rightly repelled by military regimentation. Yet there is another side as well, summed up by Woodrow Wilson:

> A friend of mine made a very poignant remark to me one day. He said: "Did you ever see a family that hung its son's yardstick or a ledger or a spade up over the mantelpiece?" But how many of you have seen the lad's rifle, his musket, hung up! Well, why? A musket is a barbarous thing. The spade and yardstick and ledger are the symbols of

peace and steady business; why not hang them up? Because they do not represent self-sacrifice. They do not glorify you in the same sense that the musket does, because when you took that musket at the call of your country you risked everything and knew you could not get anything. The most that you could do was to come back alive, but after you came back alive there was a halo about you.

5. *The draft ensures military quality.* Today the United States is a world power, caught in worldwide entanglements and commitments that may require it to put its muscle where the vital concerns of the free world are located. Yet, of all industrialized nations, we have the greatest difficulty securing military personnel. (The only NATO members without an active draft are Iceland, Luxembourg, Britain and the United States.) As a result we are getting far too many one-talented individuals when we

---

U.S. Needs Mandate A Draft

An all-volunteer force was compatible with American institutions and needs in the days when our role in world politics was small, our commitments negligible. Such is not the case today when our Navy sails the globe, when over a third of a million of our soldiers and airmen guard our European and Asian allies, and when almost as many are being prepared to fight in the Persian Gulf. To repudiate conscription under these circumstances is not merely to embrace a false notion of obligations and rights – it is to risk humiliation, needless loss of life, and perhaps catastrophe.

Eliot A. Cohen, "Why We Need A Draft," *Commentary*, April 1982.

---

need those with five and ten talents. In 1979 the intelligence levels of recruits were the lowest since the volunteer army began. In 1980 barely 50 per cent of army enlistees had high school diplomas. Moreover, the share of enlisted servicemen with some college experience has declined shockingly – from 13.9 per cent in 1964 to 3.2 per cent in 1980. Military Police at Fort Benning, Georgia, have reported lost soldiers on base asking, "How do I get back to my unit?" When asked "What is your unit?" they answer that they don't know. To the question, "What do your orders say?" they respond, "I can't read my orders. All I know is that my unit is in a big, white building."

This drop in aptitude and educational level is made especially serious by the increasing sophistication of weaponry. For example, the Black Hawk helicopter has 257 knobs and switches, 135 circuit breakers, 62 displays and 11.7 square feet of instruments and controls. "What we need is technicians," a navy commander states. Senator Sam Nunn (D., Ga.), widely respected as one of Capitol Hill's most articulate defense analysts, states, "Talk to

West Germans off the record and ask what they think of the United State's ability to fight a war. It's very, very low." . . .

6. *The draft is an appropriate response to worldly reality.* Too much antiregistration, antidraft sentiment is based on ideology rather than prudence. We have a habit of recycling anti-Vietnam rhetoric to avoid coming to terms with our proper global responsibilities. Peace advocates are prone to see the military as the bete noire and those in uniform as barbarians. They forget that both our most savage *and* our most altruistic acts have been done by those at war.

We badly need a Reinhold Niebuhr today to refresh our anthropological realism, to bring the Children of Light and the Children of Darkness of the 1980s into dialogue. If the latter need visions of hope, slight though they may be, certainly the former could use a dose of global realism. Our intellectual fare needs to be the 13th chapter of Romans as well as the Beatitudes; St. Augustine as well as St. Francis; Hobbes, Machiavelli and Lenin as well as the Berrigans and William Stringfellow.

When a registration resister says, "All war is wrong; it's far better to talk things out," I wonder who taught him world history of the 1930s and 40s. Singing for peace and cheering speakers who denounce the draft, the military, oil companies, multinational corporations and previous wars may be a good catharsis. But while the Children of Light strum guitars, others in the world are busy taking target practice.

The world, as Luther reminded us, cannot be ruled by a crucifix. Violence is endemic to the human condition, and it is globally on the increase. Only Australia, of all the continents, has been exempt from serious national or international conflict in the past few years. We must overcome our love/hate relationship with the military – embracing it in times of war, despising it in times of peace. Whatever conspiracy theories we may have about the Pentagon, however demonic we may believe the military to be, it will not, somehow, go away. What is at issue is not the fact of having a military but what kind of military is appropriate to a democratic society.

A reinstitution of the draft is not a step toward war; to see it as such is a misuse of the wedge argument. The draft is a fair and equitable means by which free people distribute the burden necessary to remain free. It will be argued that the draft is "involuntary servitude" for one or two years in order to keep the rest of life voluntary, and to ensure us against what politely has been called a "nuclear exchange."

176

"The draft is, in effect, a massive discriminatory tax on young, healthy males."

The Draft Is Unnecessary

Doug Bandow

Doug Bandow, editor of the publication *Inquiry,* formerly served as a special assistant to the President on the Committee for Policy Development. He was also a member of President Reagan's Military Manpower Task Force. In the following viewpoint, he contends that the all volunteer force (AVF) is better than reinstituting the draft. He refutes arguments against the AVF, explaining how the draft would not reduce federal spending, would not reduce overrepresentation of blacks in the army, and would not increase the overall qualifications of the recruits.

As you read, consider the following questions:

1. Why does the author believe that a draft would be more costly than a volunteer army?
2. What is the author's opinion of the large number of blacks in the military?
3. Do you agree with the author's assessment of the AVF? Why or why not?

Doug Bandow, "The Draft Has Been Proved – A Failure," *San Diego Union*, May 8, 1983. Reprinted with permission.

The volunteer military was reinaugurated a decade ago, after some 30 years of conscription. Despite voluntarism's success in meeting our national security needs, doubts about its future viability persist. The number of men turning 18 annually is falling, while the Reagan administration is expanding the military; draft registration enforcement continues. Politicians and military folks alike talk about preparing the nation for conscription. But they're wrong.

The draft is a curious institution, inconsistent with America's historical tradition of manning its armed forces with volunteers. It is also unique: No other dangerous civic service, such as police and fire departments, compels service.

This should come as no surprise. There is a reason the draft has been used so infrequently – it doesn't work very well. Critics may find it easy to attack the All Volunteer Force (AVF), but they find it much harder to show the draft to be better. Many of the standard criticisms of the AVF are incorrect; others are irrelevant or also apply to conscription.

Some have argued, for example, that the "privilege" of being an American creates some "obligation" to serve the government. But the government is the protector, not grantor, of the peoples' fundamental right to liberty; it cannot sell freedom for servitude. The nation should be defended in a manner consistent with the freedom principles upon which it was founded.

Too High a Cost

Another frequent contention is that the draft is "cheaper," since pay needn't be as high. Actually, a draft increases total social costs, and then shifts them from all taxpayers to a few draftees. The draft is, in effect, a massive discriminatory tax on young, healthy males. Additionally, all of society would pay the large cost of taking people out of their most productive civilian jobs, destabilizing the work force, and causing expensive and perverse draft avoidance activities.

In fact, a draft probably wouldn't even reduce federal spending. The U.S. spends far more than the Soviets on personnel, but most of that goes to careerists, civilians and retirees. Halving the pay of first-termers – careerists are not drafted – and eliminating all recruiting programs would save less than $4 billion. Any such savings would be offset, however, by the costs of registration, classification, induction and enforcement, and the increased careerist pay and training expenses caused by the greater turnover among draftees, who reenlist in far lower numbers than volunteers. Indeed, drafting postal workers or civilian defense

employees, terminated military retiree benefits, or confiscating ("drafting") equipment from arms manufacturers would save more money.

Another attack on the AVF is that it is "unrepresentative" of American society. What this really means is that the military is not unrepresentative in the way the critics want it to be: full or middle-class white males.

But these critics are wrong. The AVF is generally "representative" of society, especially if one looks at the military as a whole, instead of increasingly small subpopulations – the Army, first-termers, combat arms personnel, specific units. No organization in society, including the military, can be expected to be perfectly representative everywhere. (And if representativeness is so important, then how about women, middle-aged people, professionals and so on?)

When a joint Defense Department and Ohio State University study compared the military's first-term recruits to the recruits' civilian counterparts, it found that the soldiers had graduated from high school in larger numbers, had substantially higher educational aspirations and were equally well-qualified to attend college. The parents of these young service people had similar educational backgrounds, and only somewhat more blue-collar job histories, than the parents of the civilians. Moreover, half of

John Trevor, *Alberquerque Journal*. Reprinted with permission.

the military is made up of careerist officers and enlisted personnel; they fully represent mainstream America.

Blacks are overrepresented in the military – 12 percent of the population is black, compared to 19 percent of the military and 30 percent of the Army – but so what? No adverse effect has been demonstrated on the military's ability to defend America: Black soldiers are well-qualified, and there is no "white flight" from the military or even heavily black units. And since blacks freely choose to join the military, they are not bearing a "disproportionate burden" of America's defense (as they would with a draft).

But even if one believes the military has "too many" blacks, a draft is no solution. Blacks were overrepresented in the Vietnam war draft army, and the recent increase in the number of black recruits in large part has resulted from the increased educational attainment of black youth and the fact that blacks reenlist in greater numbers. A draft, to materially affect the overall composition of the military, would have to forbid all volunteers and prevent blacks from freely reenlisting. Neither policy is likely; the only time volunteers have been barred was for a short time in World War I, to keep high quality people "needed elsewhere" out of the military.

Some AVF critics question whether the military can fight. There is no direct measure of fighting ability, so we have to rely on surrogate measures, such as the Armed Forces Qualification Test (AFQT). For example, in fiscal year 1981, more of the military's recruits scored above average on the AFQT than did their civilian counterparts. Army recruits did somewhat less well, but they included no one from the lowest mental category. And even if recruit scores are considered to be too low, only a 100 percent draft would significantly reduce the number of Army recruits in the lower mental categories and increase those in the higher ones.

Superiority of Volunteers

Discipline is better, with the number of desertions, absences without leave, courts-martial and non-judicial punishments down. Though there is anecdotal evidence to suggest that the AVF can't fight, there is plenty of anecdotal evidence to the contrary (and American officers have doubted the quality of their troops throughout American history).

Moreover, volunteers are superior to draftees in their attitudes and motivation. The AVF utilizes a variety of incentives, including both patriotism and pay, to allow those who most want to

serve to do so; there is no reason those defending our nation should feel a need to rely on food stamps. In contrast, a draft merely lumps the unwilling with the willing. In fact, military expert B. H. Liddell Hart opposed the draft in wartime for this reason, writing in World War II that "Success (in modern warfare) increasingly depends on individual initiative, which in turn springs from a sense of personal responsibility – these senses are atrophied by compulsion."

Another criticism of the AVF is that the military has a shortage of skilled and experienced service people. But only a draft for life could bring in experienced and skilled careerists. Indeed, build-

---

War Resisters League Statement On the Draft

We affirm that in the nuclear age there is no effective military defense of this country and we therefore commit ourselves to exploring nonviolent means to resolve conflict, to resist oppression, and to create a society of justice with freedom. We draw strength from examples such as Martin Luther King, Jr.

We affirm that no State has the right to coerce citizens through military conscription or other forms of universal and compulsory service.

We are united in our determination to resist efforts to register or draft the youth of this country. We reject the concept of military defense, whether through an army conscripted by the harsh reality of mass unemployment – which makes the military the only job open to many in the Black and Latino communities – or through an army directly conscripted through a draft. We are absolutely opposed to a situation where the wealthy and powerful draft the poor and politically weak.

We encourage and support all who are opposed to the draft to take one or more of the following actions, depending on their personal situation, in their nonviolent affirmation of conscience and their determination to resist:

- refuse any cooperation with either the registration or conscription process, if you are of draft age;
- actively counsel, aid, abet, and support all youth who are determined to resist the draft, and take such action as may encourage them to resist;
- consider nonviolent civil disobedience to disrupt the process of registration and render any draft or registration process null and void.

We hope that our actions will set an example to the youth in every nation in the world, as part of an international effort to end conscription and militarism in every nation. When governments will not disarm, the people must disarm the governments.

Taken from an undated War Resisters' League pamphlet, titled *Don't Go! The Case for Draft Registration Resistance.*

---

ing a qualified career force would become even more difficult with a draft, since the reenlistment rate for draftees is far below that for volunteers.

The reserves also suffer serious shortfalls, but a combination of keeping better track of all reservists, experimenting with increased enlistment incentives, lowering unnecessarily high physical standards and extending the total Military Service Obligation incurred upon enlisting would solve the problem. The reserves simply need realistic financial support and effective management, which previously has been lacking.

The AVF will face challenges in the years ahead, but those challenges can be met with a mixture of traditional incentives and innovative management. The draft harkens back to a nostalgic past that never really was, and is no solution. It would not make us more secure, but it would destroy the fundamental values that make this nation worth defending. If our society lacks the moral authority to persuade its people to freely defend it, then it lacks something that no amount of coercion can restore.

"Registration is a signal to the Kremlin that the trauma of Vietnam has not so damaged the national psyche that the US won't fight back."

The Case for Draft Registration

Lisa Myers and *The Kansas City Times*

Lisa Myers, a reporter for the *Washington Star*, emphasizes in Part I of the following viewpoint that registering for the draft is not the same as being drafted. She claims that registration is not a show of militarism; instead, it is a meaningful symbol that this nation will fight back when its interests or allies are threatened. Part II, which first appeared as an editorial in *The Kansas City Times*, explains why there is a large, inherent group within the U.S. population that resists the concept of selective service. It presents the paradox of the need for defense and the difficulty of having an army, navy and air force without people.

As you read, consider the following questions:

1. Explain two of Ms. Myers' arguments favoring registration.
2. According to *The Kansas City Times*, why would the threat of effective military force influence the Soviet Union?
3. Do you believe that registration increases respect for America and underscores its resolve to defend itself? Why or why not?

Lisa Myers, "A Giant Step Toward Equality? Excerpted from *The New Republic*, March 1, 1980. Reprinted by permission of THE NEW REPUBLIC, © 1980 The New Republic, Inc.

Kansas City Times, January 26, 1980. Reprinted with permission.

I

Registration is not the draft, nor necessarily even the harbinger of a return to peacetime conscription. Neither is it the preamble to a declaration of war. It would, however, demonstrate national resolve and willingness to sacrifice to friends as well as foes. The US has been and will be asking Western allies to go along with economic and political reprisals against the Soviet Union – measures that in some cases will entail more sacrifice from them than from us. Registration would be a meaningful symbol that this nation too will sacrifice – a fact subject to international question over the last decade. Registration is a signal to the Kremlin that the trauma of Vietnam has not so damaged the national psyche that the US won't fight back when its interests or allies are threatened.

Although in military terms registration does not improve conventional capabilities, certainly it can be viewed as part of a broader effort to enhance US readiness to respond to a national emergency. If war broke out tomorrow and [the President] ordered immediate and full mobilization, it would take more than a month before the first inductees could be processed. Right now, the Pentagon doesn't even know where to find them. Under the registration proposal, which provides a list of bodies, the first inductions would occur 13 days after mobilization.

Those who oppose registration do so largely on the ground that it is a step toward war, a show of militarism. For some reason, many of these same anti-war activists consider is dishonorable to prepare oneself for a possible conflict. That's for the warmongers, they say. They want Amtrak – to ride in the opposite direction. But it is difficult to find a war in which a country was attacked because of its nonpareil military prowess. Poland wasn't the demonstration project for every European bully since Catherine the Great because it afforded a tough match. "You noticed that the Soviets attacked Afghanistan, not China," notes one administration official.

As for young people themselves – women included – registration should prompt serious reflection of their personal obligation and commitment to country, a process missed by half a generation."

II

It is in the American character to abhor regimentation in any form, and military service, almost by definition, means discipline and a following of orders. When the military is combined with

compulsory service, then the discomfort is doubly acute. And when the plain, unavoidable facts of much of military life are added – boredom, genuine danger, lost time and a disruption of civilian plans – then the crowd of people who are not enchanted by thoughts of the draft grows.

On top of all this are the natural protective instincts of parents, a few individuals who simply cannot bear the thought of personal peril, and those who are so self-centered that they are perfectly willing for others to serve, but "not me." And of course there are the conscientious objectors who cannot kill. The real conscientious objectors are ready to perform other, onerous tasks as a substitute.

"IT ISN'T ALL A MATTER OF HONOR, COUNTRY AND PATRIOTISM. THE BOTTOM LINE IS REALLY WHAT YOU ARE PREPARED TO GIVE UP TO PRESERVE THE RIGHT TO SHAPE YOUR OWN LIFE, BE YOUR OWN PERSON AND NOT LIVE IN A SOCIETY THAT IS RULED BY FEAR."

Bob Dix, *Manchester Union Leader*. Reprinted with permission.

Thus in the United States there is a large, built-in body that tends to resist the very concept of selective service. Yet even in this era it is still very difficult to have an army, navy and air force without people. And it is ridiculous, if not suicidal, for a president of the United States to speak even softly to tyrants without the big stick of adequate armed forces to back up the talk. Of course the president does have all those nuclear missiles and bombs. But sanity requires an effective military response beyond blowing up the planet. The president must have alternatives.

And so we get back to registration for the draft. . . .

The Soviet Union is an enormously powerful totalitarian state with an urge to dominate that goes far back into history – long before the advent of a "communist" government that is only a new face on an old, aggressive tyranny.

185

The Russian people and other nationalities that make up the Soviet Union have long suffered atrocities at the hands of their own rulers that have been justified in the name of the Motherland, and this includes the deaths of literally millions of men, women and children. . . . Given the nature of a closed, controlled society and a people accustomed to extreme hardship, it should be clear that only the threat of effective military force has much meaning to such a regime. The United States does not now have an effective, conventional military force.

So consideration must be given rather quickly to questions: Is some sort of universal, two-year service that would include domestic activities possible? Is there any reason young women should not be included in registration? What exemptions should be permitted? If there is to be a draft, should it be for training purposes only, or would overseas service be a possibility?

These are all important questions, but none is so basic as the one all Americans must answer: Are we willing to go ahead with registration and a possible draft on the basis of national interests as they are perceived today? One thing to remember. The first peacetime draft of 1940 would have run out in 1941. After tumultuous debate, an extension was approved in the House of Representatives Aug. 12, 1941, by *one vote*. That was less than four months before Pearl Harbor.

"Registration is souring the country's attitudes not only toward the draft, but toward government itself."

The Case Against Draft Registration

Joseph A. Tetlow

Joseph A. Tetlow, a member of the Society of Jesus, is an associate editor of the Society's weekly magazine *America*. In this viewpoint, he refutes the premise that draft registration is necessary for rapid mobilization of U.S. forces in the event of an attack. He claims that peacetime registration saves a militarily insignificant amount of time and unnecessarily requires millions of dollars of taxpayers' money to maintain it each year.

As you read, consider the following questions:

1. According to the author, who should the government call upon in the event of a national emergency?
2. Why does the author believe that the history of the draft provides a reason for canceling peacetime registration?
3. Who does the author believe should make up a national army? What is his reason?

Joseph A. Tetlow, S.J., "President Reagan and Registration for the Draft," *America*, February 21, 1981.

During the Presidential campaign, Governor Ronald Reagan opposed peacetime registration for the draft.

His opposition had diminished by the time he fielded a question at his first press conference. He apparently still felt, as he had during the campaign, "that the advance registration . . . would not materially speed up the process if an emergency required the draft." But he claimed that his nine days in office had been spent in the Cabinet room macerating the budget, "and so I just have to tell you that we will . . . make a decision on what to do with it down the road some place.". . .

President Reagan ought to cancel it for five good reasons.

First, the registration is not what President Carter called it in January 1980, "necessary for rapid mobilization." His own Defense Secretary, Harold Brown, had denied that a few months earlier. A review of military manpower and of the Selective Service System, Mr. Brown had testified to the Senate Armed Services Committee, "does not lead to the conclusion that peacetime registration is necessary."

Just one week before President Carter's call, his Director of the Selective Service System, Bernard D. Rostker, argued the same thesis. He reported that peacetime registration would save a militarily insignificant amount of time and cause resentment; the "option chosen" by the Service was to leave registration until after a draft was legislated.

Mr. Rostker also noted that peacetime registration would cost too much, which is the second reason why an economy-minded President ought to call it off. The bill, passed by the Senate on June 12 and by the House on June 26, authorized spending $13.3 million to set up the registration, which Mr. Rostker estimates will cost $23.8 million a year to keep up. That seems a small sum next to the defense outlay of $184.4 billion for 1982, but it is as much a waste of money as the "consultants' fees" President Reagan has just pared. Its aim is swift mobilization, but it registers the wrong people for that.

Skilled Personnel Needed

Here is the third reason to end the registration. In any national emergency, Senator Charles McC. Mathias Jr. (R., Md.) argued last February in an attempt to amend the Senate bill, the services will need skilled personnel – computer experts, rocket mechanics, pilots – not untrained recruits. There are hundreds of thousands of men and women who are "skilled, able and ready to move in, and move in promptly," Senator William Proxmire (D., Wisc.) pointed out, because they have already been trained

I WANT YOU
TO THINK
BEFORE YOU REGISTER
FOR THE DRAFT

in the all-volunteer services. Where are they? The Selective Service System does not know. No one does. But they are the people a peacetime registration should identify and keep track of; they are the ones the nation would need in an emergency requiring swift mobilization.

The fourth reason for canceling peacetime registration of 18-year-old males emerges from the history of the draft. During the War of Revolution, only Virginia and Massachusetts tried a draft. George Washington's letters show the draftees' attitude toward

it: When they felt like it, they went home. During the Civil War, the draft caused the worst riots the nation has known. On July 13, 1863, for instance, rioting in New York City erupted that in four days gutted stores, burned mansions, killed hundreds and was quelled only when troops poured in to stop it. In spite of four separate draft calls, only a very small part of the Union Army was directly drafted.

Two subsequent conscriptions, however, worked well. The draft that began in 1917 supplied two-thirds of the nearly four million men who fought World War I. The draft that ran from 1940 to 1949 worked just as effectively for World War II.

The Vietnam Legacy

Very briefly after that war, the armed services were composed completely of volunteers, but the Korean War launched a very much less popular and less equitable draft in 1952. In continued

---

Prostitution and Draft Registration

How would those who justify draft registration feel if young women were required to register for prostitution service? The idea is not as far-fetched as it might sound. The reason registration for military service does not sound preposterous to us is because we have become familiar with the evil of warfare. But suppose that the government were to decide that prostitution could be "diplomacy by other means," as war has been called "diplomacy by other means." A government might pursue its foreign policy objectives by entertaining foreign diplomats with call girls. The government might require all young women to register for prostitution services. Of course, there are differences between war and prostitution. But if homocide can be put into the service of humanity, why not fornication too?

John K. Stoner, "Draft Registration Signals and Symbols," *Engage/Social Action*, February 1983.

---

through several transmogrifications until the winding down of the Vietnam War. The last call-ups were in December 1972, although registration continued until 1976.

The Vietnam War wrecked the draft. These are the entries in a dictionary of American history: *Draft cards, burning of, 1965; Draft deferments, 1967; Draft evasion, 1968*. During the last years, 40 percent of those eligible applied for Conscientious Objector status and about half of them received it, as the status was vaguely and pragmatically redefined. Even so, when the Treaty of Paris was signed on Jan. 27, 1973, more than 60,000 Americans had fled the draft to Canada and Europe; 200,000 had failed to register and been referred to the Justice Department for

prosecution as felons; another quarter of a million had failed to register but were not prosecuted.

The bitterness and confusion have by no means worn away entirely. An astonishing number of secular, denominational, ecumenical and interfaith groups swiftly organized between January and July 1980 to counsel conscientious objectors. Many denominations followed the Society of Friends and the Lutherans in taking some official stand on conscientious objection, and 36 religious leaders, including five Catholic bishops, denounced the peacetime registration as "a continued attempt to militarize the American conscience."

That charge may or may not be true, and, if it is true, the attempt may or may not succeed, but if the present poorly enforced registration continues, it is more likely to aggravate the American conscience and build up the resentments that Mr. Rostker predicted. What reaction does American history suggest to the next draft: willing, like the reactions to the drafts of 1917 and 1940? Or rather recalcitrant, like those to the drafts of the War of Rebellion and the Civil War? It depends a good deal on how any future conflict begins, of course, and on how clear and compelling the cause of the United States is. But it also depends on a clear national perception that the draft is not only necessary but also equitable. The peacetime registration is likely to cloud those perceptions.

And this raises the final reason why Mr. Reagan ought to cancel the peacetime registration. It is souring the country's attitudes not only toward the draft, but toward government itself. Probably a quarter of a million have refused or neglected to register. They are thereby felons, liable to five years in prison and a $10,000 fine. . . .

A Sensible Alternative

Furthermore, half of those who ought to be eligible in some sense, American women, have been deliberately cut out of the registration by Congressional action. A great number of them will not be mollified, and the American Civil Liberties Union has taken its case against the constitutionality of an all-male registration to the Supreme Court.

In a sense, this peacetime registration does not show the "national will" Mr. Carter said it would show. It shows the Government's willingness to enact a law which is inequitable and feckless. Such a law should be wiped out.

Contrary to the intense convictions of the Founding Fathers, the country now has a standing army. During more than a

generation, it has caused all the problems the Fathers foresaw – huge expense, inequitable burdens, willful bureaucracy among them – even though the reasons against having a standing army have grimly altered.

If we must have this quasi-fourth branch of government, then it should be what it is at present, all volunteer. In that case, the only sane kind of peacetime registration is a clear record of all alumni and alumnae of that volunteer service – and a clear notice that those who have resigned from it will be called to serve in any national emergency, having volunteered themselves in the first place.

"It is time for this nation to realize that the AVF has not worked because it cannot work."

The All Volunteer Force Is a Failure

Robin L. Beard

Robin Beard, a former congressman from Tennessee, was recently appointed Deputy Secretary General of NATO Forces in Europe by President Reagan. His appointment is waiting for Senate confirmation. Mr. Beard claims that the AVF has weakened American forces since it was instituted in 1973. In the following viewpoint, Mr. Beard claims that a strong economy in the coming years will make it even more difficult for the AVF to compete for the diminishing numbers of available young men.

As you read, consider the following questions:

1. What does the author mean by "checkbook patriotism"?
2. According to the author, what is the condition of America's reserve forces?
3. What is the Skills Qualifications Test?
4. What arguments does the author offer in summary against the All-Volunteer Force?

Robin L. Beard, "The All-Volunteer Army: It Hasn't Worked — It Can't Work," *Human Events*, November 21, 1981. Reprinted with permission.

193

The recent furor over how to modernize our strategic nuclear forces has obscured for the moment what I believe to be the most fundamental of all our national defense problems: the complete inability of an all-volunteer system to provide an adequate number of men and women who are capable of operating and maintaining our modern weapons.

In 1973 this nation ended the draft and instituted the All-Volunteer Force (AVF). After eight years of the AVF, I believe it to be an unequivocal failure. Not only do I believe that the AVF has not worked, I do not believe that it can ever work, regardless of the amount of money poured into pay and recruiting. "Checkbook patriotism" will not solve our problems, even if we make the assumption that we could afford it.

The skilled, mid-career, non-commissioned officers who form the backbone of any military organization are leaving in droves, and not just because of pay problems. The junior enlisted personnel in the front-line combat units – the troops who will actually do the fighting – are, to an unacceptably high degree, comprised of America's poor and poorly educated.

We face a situation in which the casualty lists from the first few weeks of the next war will show the majority of the dead and wounded to be poor blacks and Hispanics; in other words, those with the least stake in our society will be paying the highest price to defend it. That is simply not an acceptable situation in a democracy.

The AVF is a failure simply in terms of numbers. It has neither attracted enough reruits nor retained enough career NCOs and junior officers to do its job in a major war.

This failure shows up worst of all in the Army: The Army has reduced its standards so much under the AVF concept that currently more than one out of every three recruits drops out before completing his first term of enlistment. This phenomenon obviously complicates the numbers problem, because not only is the Army falling short of recruiting goals, but many of the soldiers it does recruit wash out in their initial term. . . .

Even more important than overall manpower shortages, the people who make the Army work – the skilled NCOs – are in critically short supply in the combat units. Stateside units are so short of NCOs that the Army was recently forced to transfer several thousand back from Europe. The Army is also 28 per cent short of needed junior officers. It is indeed a "hollow Army," as Army Chief of Staff Gen. E. C. Meyer has so aptly characterized it.

Personnel Problems

The other branches are not free of critical personnel problems either. The Navy, Marines and Air Force are all facing mounting shortages of pilots,· air traffic controllers, avionics and radar specialists, jet mechanics and flight line personnel. . . .

This lack of skilled supervisory personnel has already delayed, and in some cases canceled, ship deployments. Others have deployed with less than a full complement. At a time when the Reagan Administration is rightly planning to increase the fleet by over 100 ships, we cannot even adequately man the ones we now deploy.

All of the services are suffering severe shortages of doctors. This is perhaps the cruelest and most morale-damaging shortage of all, because a lack of doctors means the serviceman too often finds that his family does not receive adequate and timely medical care. As the shortage of physicians grows, those remaining must shoulder an ever increasing workload, thus increasing their propensity to leave the service as soon as possible. . . .

However damaging these medical shortages are to morale, they should also be considered within the context of the primary mission of maintaining the health of the troops in wartime. If the military medical community does not have adequate manpower to prevent infectious diseases or quickly treat the wounded, combat commanders will soon face precarious shortages of troops. . . .

The numerical shortages in the military place a heavy burden on recruiters. The pressure to meet quotas has been so great in recent years that the Congress has learned of recruiters resorting to falsifying test scores and education certificates to get unqualified recruits qualified. These pressures can only get worse because the 18-to-21-year-old population will drop steadily over the coming decade, shrinking the manpower pool from which new recruits must come.

Reserve Forces Falling Behind

Both current and projected shortfalls in our active-duty forces are serious enough to call into question the ability of our military to survive heavy losses in the first weeks of a major war. But even if active-duty units manage to hold their own against the first massive onslaught, the eventual outcome of the conflict would be highly doubtful, for the reserve forces that provide the key to stopping prolonged aggression by a major power such as the Warsaw Pact, have become dangerously inadequate after eight years of the AVF.

The AVF was justified on the "total force" concept. It was understood by AVF planners that the active-duty forces would not – and could not – be maintained at numerical levels sufficient to fight a prolonged major war. In the case of such a war, the active forces were to be quickly reinforced by a trained reserve. Without that immediate reserve mobilization capacity, the AVF would not be able to fight effectively beyond the initial few weeks.

The state of the reserve forces today is frankly appalling. The organized reserves – those units that train once a month – are at

Don Hesse, *St. Louis Globe/Democrat.* Reprinted with permission.

only 85 per cent of required strength. The Army reserve, for example – which is crucial, because in a European war the Army would have the most casualties in the shortest time, thus needing the most replacements – currently stands far below its requirements.

The Individual Ready Reserve (IRR) – comprised of those who, though not members of organized reserve units, are trained and ready to be called up on short notice – is over 700,000 men short of wartime requirements. In 1973, when the AVF began, the IRR had 1.2 million members; today it has 220,000. I might add that

the IRR had fallen to 150,000 before the Army began counting first-term dropouts who had finished their basic training as part of the IRR.

Dangerous Disadvantages

These numerical problems are frightening enough, but even more threatening to the potential combat effectiveness of the AVF is the quality of the personnel who will be expected to win a war in which they will almost certainly be vastly outnumbered by both men and machines.

In any war with the Warsaw Pact, American forces would face tremendous disadvantages in numbers of tanks, planes, artillery tubes and other conventional weapons. American defense officials pray that these severe quantitative disadvantages will be offset by superior American weapons technology. But the superior technology (an assumption increasingly more tenuous) is highly complex and difficult to operate and maintain (itself a subject of concern). . . .

Technologically superior weaponry is useless without personnel who are able to operate and maintain it. The unimpeachable fact is that the AVF does not have enough capable personnel.

The armed forces classify recruits into four categories of intellectual ability based on entrance examination scores. Category IV is the lowest range of scores that allows an individual to enter the military. Those who score in Category IV come from the lower 30 per cent in intelligence test scores of the overall American population.

After four years of denials, former Assistant Secretary of Defense for Manpower Robert Pirie admitted last year that the percentage of Category IVs among recruits was far higher than previously admitted by the Defense Department. . . .

The Army has been forced to rewrite all its training manuals at a seventh-grade level. Even so, a third of its soldiers reportedly still have difficulty comprehending them. Two per cent of the Army cannot even speak English well enough to communicate with fellow soldiers.

In the draft Army of 1965, about one-fourth were high school dropouts. Today that figure is one-half. As I have previously pointed out, one in three Army recruits is so unsatisfactory that he never manages to complete his first term of enlistment.

During his disastrous tenure as Army secretary, Clifford Alexander contended that intelligence test scores were "irrelevant" to job performance and even went so far as to order them

removed from the soldier's individual records. But the Army has examinations that are directly related to job performance. They are called Skills Qualifications Tests (SQTs) and they measure a soldier's ability to do the job to which he will be assigned in the event of war. The Army's own figures show shockingly high failure rates on SQTs. . . .

Exodus of Skilled NCOs

Thus we can see one primary cause of the exodus of skilled, mid-career NCOs from the services: their complete lack of confidence in the troops they must lead. I go on active-duty as a reservist with the Marines two weeks every year, and I have repeatedly heard NCOs and junior officers say that they were getting out because the quality of the enlisted personnel assigned to them was so poor that they simply could not adequately perform their mission. As more than one put it, "It would be suicide to go into combat depending on some of these guys."

Nor is this observation limited to my personal experience. Numerous indicators bear it out.

In an August 1979 survey of 3,000 Army officers, fully 83 per cent named the low ability of personnel under their supervision as a serious problem. Even more officers saw a problem with leadership and motivation among junior NCOs.

The Defense Department recently released a report showing that those junior enlisted personnel who scored the lowest on intelligence tests were the most likely to reenlist after their first term, thus eventually moving up into the NCO ranks to replace those now getting out. Therefore, what is occurring is that the most untrainable are becoming trainers themselves.

If one believes, as I do, that people vote with their feet, then the decline in retention rates among NCOs and junior officers is a massive vote of no confidence in the AVF by the people in the best position to know, not the generals and DOD bureaucrats, but the sergeants and lieutenants.

I would suggest it is rather naive to insist that simply raising pay will cure the retention problem. I do not doubt that drastic increases in pay will ease retention problems somewhat. The most recent statistics show better retention figures among NCOs and junior officers, due as much to a stagnant economy as higher pay, I think. Recruiting figures for the first-termers have also improved as the economy has slowed and unemployment, particularly among black youths, has risen.

But I seriously question whether this nation – which now spends over 60 per cent of its entire defense budget on pay and

benefits for personnel – can afford the regular and massive pay increases it would take to attract enough capable recruits to man our active-duty pay forces. Nor would higher active-duty pay do anything to substantially improve the state of the reserves.

As a fervent supporter of the Reagan economic plan, I also believe that the private sector boom that will surely result from his policies will make it clearly impossible for the miltary to afford to compete for adequate manpower in the next decade, a decade in which the 18-to-21 age cohort will constantly grow smaller.

'Checkbook Patriotism' Rejected

I must totally reject the argument that service in the defense of one's country is merely another commodity to be purchased in the marketplace by the government, that the government has no right to "coerce" service on the part of individuals.

This mentality is purely and simply "checkbook patriotism." It reduces those who are in the military to the level of mere government employees, who are there because they derive more economic benefit from that endeavor than from their other choices of employment – or lack of choices, as is more often the case today.

The All-Volunteer Force is actually conscription of another type – conscription by poverty. For if the private sector booms as we expect it to, only those who cannot succeed in it will opt for the military and not because they want to, but because they have to.

The All-Volunteer Force has produced and will continue to produce a complete separation of the military from the mainstream of the society it is supposed to defend. The middle and upper classes have abandoned the miltary and will continue to do so because their options in the private sector will always be more attractive.

Just how much money would it take to persuade a child of middle-class suburbia to sign up for four years of sitting in a frozen foxhole in an outpost half a world away from family and friends? There is a spiritual void in a society that refuses to spread the burden of defending itself across all its segments; it is particularly pernicious in a democracy.

It was the Nixon Administration that ended the draft. Each succeeding administration – Ford, Carter and now Reagan – has come into office saying that the AVF has not worked because it hasn't had time, or that pay hasn't been high enough and that it will do a better job of making the AVF work than its

predecessor.

I submit that it is time for this nation to realize that the AVF has not worked because it cannot work. It cannot work because America cannot afford it, not only financially, but spiritually.

"Supporters of the peacetime draft have used the All Volunteer Force as a scapegoat for our military manpower problems. It's a bum rap."

The All Volunteer Force Is Not a Failure

William L. Armstrong

William Armstrong is a republican senator representing the state of Colorado. In the following viewpoint, written for distribution to the press in late 1980, the senator claims the All Volunteer Force has not worked because it has not been given a chance. His arguments, which are echoed by draft critics today, state that retention, not recruitment, is the main problem faced by proponents of a strong military force.

As you read, consider the following questions:

1. According to the author, with what two fundamental principles of American democracy does conscription conflict?
2. According to the author, where are manpower shortages in the armed forces most severe?
3. Why does the author believe that a draft will not eliminate the most severe personal shortages?
4. According to the author, how do military salaries compare with similar civilian salaries? What examples does he offer?

Press release from the office of Senator William L. Armstrong, Republican from Colorado.

H. L. Mencken said that "for every human problem, there is always an easy solution – neat, plausible, and wrong." The Sage of Baltimore could find ample evidence to support his thesis in the arguments being offered by both sides in the debate that is raging now over the future of the All Volunteer Force. Few issues before Congress have generated so much heat, or so little light. . . .

The debate is especially intense because the issue of conscription appears to bring into conflict two fundamental principles of American democracy.

The first principle is liberty. Ours is a free society, populated in large part by peoples who came here to avoid conscription in their homelands. There should be no place in a free society for involuntary servitude of any kind.

The second principle is duty. Freedom isn't free. A price has to be paid to maintain it, and that price is eternal vigilance. Each citizen has an obligation to serve if his or her service is required to preserve freedom.

Also involved, of course, are the overriding issues of peace and war. There are some who believe that a strong military is a provocation which will make war more likely, but most Americans believe a strong defense is the best deterrent to war.

Any debate that involves questions of liberty and duty, peace and war, is bound to get intense and emotional. Unfortunately, in intense and emotional debates, the facts tend to get drowned in a flood of rhetoric. I think it's time we toned down the rhetoric and took a closer look at the facts. . . .

There is no question that we'll need a draft if the U.S. is unfortunate enough to get involved in another war. There is simply no other way to man the force at wartime levels. The important question is whether the draft is the only way – or at least the clearly superior way – to recruit the quantity and quality of young men and women we need to maintain our peacetime defenses at required levels.

Supporters of peacetime conscription cite a rash of recent newspaper and magazine articles bemoaning the sorry state of our armed forces today as proof positive of the failure of the All Volunteer Force. . . .

Something *is* terribly wrong. The manpower crisis is even worse than most supporters of the draft suspect. The Army admitted recently that six of its 10 divisions in the continental U.S. are unready for combat, and only one of these divisions – the 82nd Airborne – is fully ready to fight. The Army's dismal report was followed a week later by the Navy's confession that

only six of its 13 aircraft carriers, and barely 94 of its 155 aircraft squadrons, were combat ready.

A number of factors contribute to this abysmal state of readiness. Among them are shortages of weapons, spare parts, fuel, ammunition, and transport. However, the greatest cause by far is a shortage of people, especially of people with the skill and experience necessary to operate the sophisticated hardware our defense depends upon today.

Personnel Shortages

The Congressionally authorized strengths of our armed forces are at their lowest levels since 1950, yet all of the services have been unable to meet those end strengths. Along with difficulty in attracting new recruits, the armed forces are discovering that a steadily increasing percentage of those they do recruit are unsuitable for military service and must be discharged before their term of enlistment expires.

In addition to the decline in the number of volunteers, there has been an even more disturbing decline in their aptitude. The number of high school graduates enlisting has plunged precipitously since the early years of the All Volunteer Force, and an increasing proportion of the high school graduates have come from the bottom half of their classes. Army manuals have been rewritten downward to eighth- and even seventh-grade levels, and still commanders report many soldiers have difficulty comprehending them.

Personnel shortages have become so severe it is becoming doubtful that our armed forces can perform adequately their peacetime missions, to say nothing of their wartime missions. Some combat units in "active" Army divisions have been "zeroed out" in order to build up other units in the same divisions to the minimum strength necessary for combat effectiveness. The Navy recently had to tie up a front-line ship, the oiler *U.S.S. Canisteo*, for lack of skilled sailors to man it, and more ships are on their way to the beach. Many front-line Air Force fighters are grounded because maintenance crews lack the experience to keep them in flying condition.

Worse, the Army's recently inaugurated Skill Qualification Tests (SQT's) seem to indicate that a very large proportion of the soldiers who are in the field are unable to do their jobs properly. Of artillery crewmen tested, 85% failed. The failure rate for tracked vehicle mechanics was 89%; for nuclear weapons maintenance specialists, 90%; and for tank turret and artillery repairmen, 98%. The Army points out, correctly, that the low scores on these SQT's are due more to the way the tests were

designed and to inadequate training than to recruit aptitude, but a failure rate of that magnitude clearly is cause for alarm.

The solution, critics of the All Volunteer Force say, is to restore peacetime conscription. In addition to solving the manpower shortage, bringing back the draft would raise the aptitude level of the armed forces, make them more representative of society as a whole, reinstill patriotism and a sense of national purpose in America's youth, reassure our allies, and fire a warning shot across the Soviet bow.

There you have it: an easy solution that is neat, plausible – and wrong. When we take a closer look at the facts, the case for resumption of the peacetime draft melts away.

Our military manpower problems are bad, and they are getting worse, but there is no evidence to indicate resumption of the peacetime draft would solve the most severe of these problems, and much evidence to indicate that it would not.

The Retention Problem

To begin with, the lion's share of the military manpower problem is a problem of retention, not recruitment. Manpower shortages are most severe in the middle officer and noncommissioned officer grades, especially in the combat arms and in highly skilled military occupations such as pilots and nuclear submariners. . . .

A draft can prevent a shortage of privates and the existence of a draft can prevent a shortage of second lieutenants, but a draft can do nothing to prevent a shortage of corporals and sergeants, captains and majors – and it is the corporals and the sergeants, the captains and the majors, that we lack. The armed forces as a whole were actually *overstrength* last year in the draftable and draft-influenced pay grades.

The cause of the sharp decline in retention is no secret, and it has nothing whatever to do with whether or not a soldier or sailor or airman enters the Armed Forces as a volunteer or as a draftee. The grim truth is that retention rates have sunk to red alert levels because Congress permitted military pay and benefits to sink so low that patriotic, motivated, dedicated men and women literally can no longer afford to serve their country.

Regular military compensation – base pay plus allowances for housing and food – has fallen more than 20% relative to the cost of living since the All Volunteer Force came into being eight years ago. Many specialty and hazardous duty pays have not been adjusted upward since 1955.

The effect of this neglect of the members of the Armed Forces

has been catastrophic. An E-4 plane handler on an aircraft carrier works about 100 hours a week and is separated from his family for from six to nine months a year; yet, he earns less than a cashier at a fast-food restaurant on a 40-hour week. A cook or a boiler technician of a ship in the Indian Ocean earns half as much as his civilian counterpart, who goes home to his wife and children each night. A sergeant E-5 with a wife and two children to support would be eligible for food stamps at most posts in the U.S. A chief petty officer with 17 years of experience earns no more than a janitor on the union scale. . . .

The servicemen I've talked to who are getting out after seven, 10, and even 15 years of service don't want to take off their uniforms. They're proud of their country and proud of their role in defending her, but patriotism doesn't put food on the table or buy shoes for the children. A serviceman today knows his family is going to have to do without the amenities civilians take for granted. He's forced to choose between his duty to his country and his duty to his family. Given the circumstances, the wonder is not that so many are leaving – the wonder is that so many are staying.

Our present military manpower problem is caused by a shortage of skilled manpower with five to 15 years of experience. There is no possible way that drafting untrained boys and girls for two years of service or less can solve this problem. There can be no solution to the military manpower problem that does not address the problem of retention, and there can be no solution to the problem of retention that does not involve a substantial increase in pay and benefits. Congress must redeem the promises it made – and subsequently broke – to keep the earnings of military personnel roughly comparable to those of their counterparts in the civilian world.

The draft is unable to solve the retention problem and unneeded to prevent a shortage of recruits if the retention problem were solved, since recruiting shortfalls over the last several years were the result of unreasonably high demands imposed by abysmal rates of retention. Surely, the draft would raise the aptitude level of recruits, and make them more representative of society as a whole? Yes – but far less effectively, and at much greater expense, than this could be accomplished by voluntary means.

Even if no effort is made to solve the retention problem, the number of draftees required to bring the armed forces up to present authorized strengths is relatively trivial. Fifty-thousand draftees a year would put an end to present shortages and permit

the Armed Forces to replace 20,000 volunteers in the lowest mental category with draftees of greater aptitude.

Before any could be drafted, however, all would have to be registered, classified, and examined. This isn't cheap. It would cost upwards of $500,000,000 a year, even before the first draftee reported for basic training. The only way in which the enormous start-up costs involved in a draft could be recouped is if a very large number of young men were to be drafted.

Since draftees would represent a cross-section of society, they would tend to raise the over-all aptitude level of the armed forces, which is currently below the national mean. Yet, even if we are only going to be injecting 50,000 "average" recruits a year into a military establishment of 2,100,000 persons and going to turn that 50,000 over every two years, it could take well into the next century before any significant improvement is seen in force "quality."

There is a faster and cheaper way.

Termination of the G.I. Bill

The All Volunteer Force concept is no more to blame for the decline in recruit aptitude than it is for the problem of retention. The big drop in the number of recruits scoring high on the armed forces mental test didn't take place after the draft ended in 1973; it happened after Congress terminated eligibility for G.I. Bill education benefits in December, 1976, despite the fact that the Army had warned Congress what would happen.

In September, 1974, the Army conducted a survey of 11,336 recruits at Armed Forces Entrance Examining Stations throughout the U.S. Twenty-four per cent said flatly they would not have enlisted if there had been no G.I. Bill. An additional 36% said they weren't sure they'd have enlisted or not if they hadn't been made eligible for education benefits. After factoring out the indifferents, the Army concluded that termination of the G.I. Bill could depress the pool of potential recruits by as much as 36.7% – all right off the top.

That wasn't all. In its report to the Secretary of Defense, the Army said terminating the G.I. Bill would require a 17% increase in annual accessions just to offset the increased losses in attrition (servicemen discharged before their term of enlistment expires) the Army could expect as a result of drawing a disproportionate number of recruits from the lower mental categories.

This grim Army prognosis seems rosy in hindsight. The number of those in the highest mental category enlisting in the Army

has dropped by two-thirds since termination of the G.I. Bill, and the number of volunteers in the second highest mental category has been cut in half. The attrition rate has climbed to nearly 40%, rather than the 18% the Army predicted Congress would find "unacceptable."

The best way to undo the damage done by cancellation of the G.I. Bill is to reinstate the G.I. Bill, not the draft. Properly tailored educational incentives almost certainly will bring into the Armed Forces at least 50,000 high-quality recruits, enough to resolve present recruiting shortfalls and to replace 15-20,000 enlistees from the lowest mental category with volunteers from the highest categories.

An injection of 50,000 high-quality recruits each year would raise aptitude levels in the armed forces far faster than would the draft, which would bring in only an average cross-section of the youth population. Moreover, a G.I. Bill would bring them in at far less cost, since there would be no need for registration or classification, and only those volunteering would require medical exams.

Supporters of the peacetime draft have used the All Volunteer Force as a scapegoat for our military manpower problems. It's a bum rap. The real culprit is a Congress which pays career servicemen so little they have to obtain food stamps to feed their families, which terminated the G.I. Bills, and which continually cuts funds for training.

The All Volunteer Force hasn't failed us. We have failed the All Volunteer Force.

Understanding Words in Context

Readers occasionally come across words which they do not recognize. And frequently, because the reader does not know a word or words, he or she will not fully understand the passage being read. Obviously, the reader can look up an unfamiliar word in a dictionary. However, by carefully examining the word in the context in which it is used, the word's meaning can often be determined. A careful reader may find clues to the meaning of the word in surrounding words, ideas and attitudes.

Below are ten excerpts from the viewpoints in this chapter. In each excerpt, one or two words are printed in italics. Try to determine the meaning of each word by reading the excerpt. Under each excerpt you will find four definitions for the italicized word. Choose the one that is closest to your understanding of the word.

Finally, use a dictionary to see how well you have understood the words in context. It will be helpful to discuss with others the clues which helped you decide each word's meaning.

1. Racial *DEMOGRAPHICS* makes very clear the mercenary nature of the "volunteer" military. A recent Brookings Institute study reveals that 33 percent of the army and 22 percent of the Marine Corps is black.

   DEMOGRAPHICS means
   a) quotas   b) statistical studies
   c) politicians   d) financial policies

2. Some liberals are *ETHICALLY MYOPIC* in not seeing the injustice of the mercenary nature of our military.

   ETHICALLY MYOPIC means
   a) unusually conservative   b) racially prejudiced
   c) morally blind   d) irrationally angry

3. Violence is *ENDEMIC* to the human condition, and it is globally on the increase. Only Australia has been exempt from serious conflict in the past few years.

ENDEMIC means
a) a natural part of
b) destructive
c) offensive
d) terminal

4. In fact, military expert B.H. Liddell Hart opposed the draft in wartime for this reason. "Success (in modern warfare) increasingly depends on individual initiative, which in turn springs from a sense of personal responsibility – these senses are *ATRO-PHIED* by compulsion.

ATROPHIED means
a) increased
b) deteriorated
c) improved
d) made more personal

5. But it is difficult to find a war in which a country was attacked because of its *NONPAREIL* military *PROWESS*. Poland wasn't the demonstration project for every European bully since Catherine the Great because it afforded a tough match.

NONPAREIL means
a) outstanding
b) inferior
c) not parallel
d) wishy-washy

PROWESS means
a) weakness
b) pride
c) inferior to technique
d) superior skill

6. It is in the American character to *ABHOR* regimentation in any form, and military service, almost by definition, means discipline and a following of orders. When the military is combined with compulsory service, then the discomfort is doubly acute.

ABHOR means
a) admire
b) hate
c) be fascinated by
d) be efficient at

7. Furthermore, half of those who ought to be eligible in some sense have been deliberately cut out of the registration by Congressional action. A great number of them will not be *MOLLIFIED*, and the American Civil Liberties Union has taken their case to the Supreme Court.

MOLLIFIED means
a) angered, maddened
b) eligible, qualified
c) satisfied, appeased
d) frustrated, upset

Appendixes

Organizations to Contact

American Enterprise Institute for Policy Research
1150 17th Street N.W.
Washington, DC 20036
(202) 862-5800

The Institute, founded in 1943, is a conservative think tank that researches a number of issues, including foreign policy and defense. A subscription to *Foreign Policy and Defense Review*, published bi-monthly, costs $18 a year.

Americanism Educational League
P.O. Box 5986
Buena Park, CA 90622
(714) 828-5040

The League, founded in 1927, campaigns on behalf of private ownership of property, strong national defense, strict crime control and limited government conducted within balanced budgets. It periodically publishes position papers and pamphlets on national defense issues.

American Friends Service Committee
1501 Cherry Street
Philadelphia, PA 19102
(215) 241-7000

The Religious Society of Friends (Quakers) founded the Committee in 1917, but it is supported and staffed by individuals of all major denominations. Its purpose is to relieve human suffering and to find new approaches to world peace and nonviolent social change. It is a co-recipient of the Nobel Peace Prize.

American Security Council
Washington Communications Center
Boston, VA 22713
(703) 825-8336

The Council was founded in 1955 to support national research and information on national security. It maintains a Washington bureau and broadcasts Radio Free Americas, a daily Spanish language program on over 38 stations throughout the Americas. It organizes and serves as program secretariat for Coalition for Peace Through Strength, and publishes two monthlies, the *Coalition Insider* and *Washington Report*.

Agency for Military and Draft Counseling
2208 South Street
Philadelphia, PA 19146
(215) 545-4626

Formerly the Central Committee for Conscientious Objectors, this agency assists persons "who find themselves facing conflict with the power of the

state" because of their opposition to the military. It publishes the *Counter-Pentagon*, *News Notes*, and numerous books and pamphlets.

Center for Defense Information
Capitol Gallery West
600 Maryland Avenue S.W.
Washington, DC 20024
(202) 484-9490

The Center, founded in 1972, as a non-partisan research organization, provides up-to-date information and analyses of the U.S. military. A subscription to *The Defense Monitor*, published ten times a year, is included in its annual $25 membership fee.

Center for International Policy
120 Maryland Avenue N.E.
Washington, DC 20002
(202) 544-4666

This project of Fund for Peace is intended to examine the impact of U.S. foreign policy on human rights and social and economic needs in the Third World. It sponsors the Indochina Project, which examines U.S. policy toward Vietnam, Laos, and Kampuchea. Its publications are *Indochina Issues* and the *International Policy Report*.

Christian Anti-Communist Crusade
P.O. Box 890
227 E. Sixth Street
Long Beach, CA 90801
(213) 437-0941

The Crusade, founded in 1953, sponsors anti-subversive seminars "to inform Americans of the philosophy, morality, organization, techniques and strategy of Communism and associated forces." Its newsletter, published semi-monthly, is free.

Coalition for a New Foreign and Military Policy
120 Maryland Avenue N.E.
Washington, DC 20002
(202) 546-8400

The Coalition, founded in 1976, united 44 national religious, labor, peace, research and social action organizations working for a "peaceful, non-interventionist and demilitarized U.S. foreign policy." It works to reduce military spending, protect human rights and promote arms control and disarmament. A subscription to *Coalition Close-Up*, published quarterly, and other publications, is included in its annual $20 membership fee.

Committee On the Present Danger
1800 Massachusetts Avenue N.E.
Washington, DC 20036
(202) 466-7444

The Committee, founded in 1976, describes its functions as directing attention to the unfavorable military balance between the United States and the Soviet Union. It publishes occasional papers dealing with this issue.

Congressional Budget Office
Office of Intergovernmental Relations
House Annex #2
2nd and D Streets S.W.
Washington, DC 20515

The CBO is an agency of Congress established to review the budgetary implications of various programs. Budget issue papers consider a host of narrow issues, but also very broad strategic analyses. Write for a list of publications. All CBO publications can be received free.

Council for a Livable World
100 Maryland Avenue N.E.
Washington, DC 20002
(202) 543-4100

The Council, founded in 1962, is a public interest group which raises funds for Senatorial candidates who work for arms control, and which lobbies on arms control and military budget issues. It publishes study papers and fact sheets on issues of foreign policy and arms control.

Council for the Defense of Freedom
P.O. Box 28526
Washington, DC 20005
(202) 783-6736

The Council, founded in 1951, is concerned about "the mortal danger we face if we do not stop communist aggression." Its weekly paper, *The Washington Inquirer*, repeatedly deals with the arms race and "our failure to take measures to overcome our lack of preparedness." A subscription is $20 a year.

Council On Economic Priorities
84 Fifth Avenue
New York, NY 10011
(212) 691-8550

The Council, founded in 1969, disseminates information on a number of economic issues, including military contracting and spending. Its newsletter, published eight to twelve times a year, is included in its annual membership fee of $15 a year. Students may join for $7.50 a year. Also included with membership are several studies and reports.

Department of Defense
Office of Public Affairs
Public Correspondence Division
Room 2E 777
Washington, DC 20037

Write for a list of publications and an order form.

Disarm Education Fund
113 University Place
New York, NY 10003
(212) 475-3232

The Fund was founded in 1976 to promote international peace, social justice,

and self-determination through opposition of military intervention, nuclear arms, and U.S. first strike capability. It supports a demilitarized foreign policy and believes that freedom from war is a fundamental human right.

Fellowship of Reconciliation
Box 271
Nyack, NY 10960
(914) 358-4601

FOR, founded in 1915, is a pacifist organization, made up of religious pacifists drawn from all faiths. It "attempts, through education and action, to substitute nonviolence and reconciliation for violence in international relations." It publishes pamphlets, books, cards and the monthly *Fellowship* dealing with disarmament and nonviolence. A subscription to *Fellowship* is $6 a year.

Foreign Policy Association
205 Lexington Avenue
New York, NY 10016
(212) 481-8450

The Association, founded in 1918, is a non-partisan educational organization that deals with foreign policy issues. It publishes a wide range of publications dealing with foreign policy.

The Heritage Foundation
513 C Street N.E.
Washington, DC 20002
(202) 546-4400

The Foundation, founded in 1974, is "dedicated to limited government, individual and economic freedom and a strong national defense." It publishes research in various formats on national defense. A subscription to *National Security Record*, published monthly, is $25 a year.

Institute for Defense and Disarmament Studies
251 Harvard Street
Brookline, MA 92146
(617) 734-4216

The Institute, incorporated in 1980, was founded "to study the nature and purposes of military forces and the obstacles to and opportunities for disarmament." It publishes an annual survey of *World Military Forces & Disarmament Opportunities* and other disarmament materials.

Institute for Policy Studies
1901 Q Street N.W.
Washington, DC 20009
(202) 234-9382

The Institute, founded in 1963, is a research and public education center which publishes a variety of books, reports and issues papers on international affairs. Write for a catalog of its publications.

Pax Christi USA
6337 W. Cornelia Avenue
Chicago, IL 60634
(312) 736-2114

Founded in 1973, Pax Christi is a Roman Catholic peace movement, dedicated to "building peace and justice by exploring and articulating the ideal of Christian nonviolence." It works for disarmament, a just world order, selective conscientious objection, education for peace and alternatives to violence. It publishes occasional papers and a quarterly newsletter which can be obtained by making a voluntary contribution.

Soviet Embassy
Information Department
1706 18th Street N.W.
Washington, DC 20009

Speeches and statements on disarmament and Soviet foreign policy are available. It is best to ask for a specific speech or publication.

U.S. Government Accounting Office
Document Handling and Information Services Facility
P.O. Box 6015
Gaithersburg, MD 20760

The GAO reviews the general efficiency of government administration and particular procurement programs. It is a good source of authoritative critiques of Pentagon programs. Write for the *Monthly List of GAO Reports*, which includes an order form. A single copy of any GAO report is free.

War Resisters League
339 Lafayette Street
New York, NY 10012
(212) 228-0450

WRL, founded in 1923, is a national pacifist organization opposed to armaments, conscription and war. *WRL News*, published every other month, is free. *Win* magazine is $20 a year.

World Policy Institute
777 United Nations Plaza
New York, NY 10017
(212) 490-0010

The Institute is a pioneer organization in research and development of a peace and world order curriculum for the college and university level. It publishes the *Journal of World Policy*, and the *Bulletin of Peace Proposals*.

Women's International League for Peace and Freedom
1213 Race Street
Philadelphia, PA 19107
(215) 563-7110

The League, founded in 1915, is made up of women interested in achieving, by nonviolent means, "freedom from fear of war, of want and of discrimination on any basis." The League supports total, universal disarmament. It maintains a legislative office in Washington DC and publishes *Legislative Bulletin, Peace and Freedom,* and *Program Action Newsletter,* in addition to pamphlets and leaflets.

Bibliography

BOOKS

Stephen E. Ambrose & James A. Barber, Jr., eds.	*The Military and American Society*. New York: The Free Press, 1972.
Martin Anderson, ed.	*The Military Draft*. Stanford, CA: Stanford University/Hoover Institute Press, 1982.
	Registration and the Draft. Stanford, CA: Stanford University/Hoover Institute Press, 1982.
Richard J. Barnet	*Real Security: Restoring American Power in a Dangerous Decade*. New York: Simon & Schuster, 1981.
Jason Berger, ed.	*The Military Draft*. New York: H. W. Wilson Company, 1981.
Boston Study Group	*Winding Down: The Price of Defense*. San Francisco: Boston Study Group, 1982.
Harold Brown	*Thinking About National Security*. Boulder, CO: Westview Press, 1983.
James Chance	*Solvency: The Price of Survival*. New York: Random House, 1981.
Andrew Cockburn	*The Threat: Inside the Soviet Military Machine*. New York: Random House, 1983.
Congressional Quarterly	*U.S. Defense Policy*. Washington, DC: Congressional Quarterly, 1980.
Congressional Research Service	*Should the United States Significantly Increase Its Foreign Military Commitments?* Washington, DC: U.S. Government Printing Office, 1980. (An anthology of alternative views.)
Robert W. DeGrasse, Jr.	*Military Expansion, Economic Decline*. New York: Council on Economic Priorities, 1983.
Theodore Draper	*Defending America*. New York: Basic Books, 1977.
Thomas H. Etzold	*Defense or Delusion?* New York: Harper & Row, 1982.
James Fallows	*National Defense*. New York: Random House, 1981.
Peter Karsten, ed.	*The Military in America*. New York: The Free Press, 1980.
Christopher A. Kojn, ed.	*U.S. Defense Policy*. Chicago: H.W. Wilson Company, 1982.
Sidney Lens	*The Maginot Line Syndrome*. Cambridge, MA: Ballinger, 1983.

216

Walter Millis, ed.	*American Military Thought.* New York: Bobbs-Merrill Company, 1966.
Daniel O'Graham	*Shall America Be Defended?* New Rochelle, NY: Arlington House, 1979.
W. Scott Thomson, ed.	*From Weakness to Strength: National Security in the 1980's.* San Francisco: Institute for Contemporary Studies, 1980.
Sheila Tobias, et al	*What Kinds of Guns Are They Buying for Your Butter?* New York: William Morrow, 1983.
Caspar W. Weinberger	*Annual Report to the Congress.* Washington, DC: Superintendent of Documents, 1983.
Ronald A. Wells, ed.	*The Wars of America – Christian Views.* Grand Rapids, Michigan: William B. Eerdmans, 1981.
Western Goals	*The War Called Peace: The Soviet Peace Offensive.* Alexandria, Virginia: Western Goals, 1982.

PAMPHLETS

AFL-CIO	*Action/Defense Report.* AFL-CIO, 1983. Available free from AFL-CIO, 815 Sixteenth St., NW, Washington, D.C. 20006.
American Friends Service Committee	*Questions & Answers on the Soviet Threat and National Security.* AFSC, 1982. Available for $1.00 from AFSC, 1501 Cherry St., Philadelphia, PA 19102.
Marion Anderson	*The Empty Pork Barrel.* Employment Research Associates, 1982. Available for $2.00 from Employment Research Associates, 400 South Washington Ave., Lansing, Michigan 48933. Ask for price list of similar publications.
Jeffrey G. Barlow, ed.	*Reforming the Military.* The Heritage Foundation, 1981. Available for $3.00 from The Heritage Foundation. Ask for price list of similar publications.
Committee on the Present Danger	*Is the Reagan Defense Program Adequate?* Committee on the Present Danger, 1982. Available free from the Committee on the Present Danger, 1028 Connecticut Ave., NW, Washington, D.C. 20036. Ask for price list of similar publications.
Congressional Budget Office	*Defense Spending and the Economy.* Congressional Budget Office, 1983. Available free from The Superintendent of Documents, U.S. Government Printing Office, Washington, D.C. 20402.

217

Robert DeGrasse & Others *The Costs and Consequences of Reagan's Military Buildup.* The Council of Economic Priorities, 1982. Available for $2.50 from the Council on Economic Priorities, 84 Fifth Ave., New York, NY 10011.

Department of Defense *Soviet Military Power.* Department of Defense, 1983. Available for $6.50 from Superintendent of Documents, U.S. Government Printing Office, Washington, D.C. 20402.

Samuel T. Francis *The Soviet Strategy of Terror.* The Heritage Foundation, 1981. Available for $2.00 from the Heritage Foundation, same as above.

Fred Charles Ikle *What It Means to Be Number Two.* Ethics and Public Policy Center, undated. Available for $1.00 from Ethics and Public Policy Center, 1211 Connecticut Ave., NW, Washington, D.C. 20036.

Steve Meiers, ed. *Basic Training: A Consumer's Guide to the Military.* The Progressive Foundation, 1982. Available for $2.95 from The Progressive Foundation, 350 W. Gorham St., Madison, Wisconsin 53703.

National Conference of Catholic Bishops *The Challenge of Peace: God's Promise and Our Response.* NC Documentary Service, 1983. Available for $3.50 from the National Catholic News Service, 1312 Massachusetts Ave., NW, Washington, D.C. 20005.

Ruth Leger Sivard *Military Budgets and Social Needs: Setting World Priorities.* Public Affairs Committee, 1977. Available for 50¢ from Public Affairs Pamphlets, 381 Park Ave., S., New York, NY 10016.

World Military and Social Expenditures 1982. World Priorities, 1982. Available for $4.00 from World Priorities, Box 1003, Leesburg, Virginia 22075.

MAGAZINES

Gordon Adams "Congress Begins the Debate," *The Bulletin of the Atomic Scientists,* April 1983, p. 25.

Joseph P. Addabbo "Is the High Cost of Defense Spending Justified? No," *USA Today,* September 1982, p. 14.

The American Legion "Should U.S. Forces Stationed in Europe Be Reduced?" November 1982, p. 10.

Bill Armstrong "Volunteer Armed Forces: A Senator's View," *National Review,* March 6, 1981, p. 215.

Doug Bandow   "Freedom, the Draft and the AVF," *Inquiry*, April
                               1983, p. 36.

                               "The Volunteer Military: A Moral and Practical
                               Imperative," *New Guard*, Winter 1982-1983, p.
                               16.

Richard Barnet   "Of Cables and Crises," *Sojourners*, February
                               1983, p. 16.

Srully Blotnick   "Cosmetic Bookkeeping," *Forbes*, April 25, 1983,
                               p. 198.

V. Boikov   "Bankrolling the Pentagon," *World Press
                               Review*, March 1981, p. 47.

Arnaud de Borchgrave   "A Strong America: Key to World Peace," *New
                               Guard*, Winter 1980-82, p. 30.

Jim Bristol   "Resisting Registration, Stopping the Draft,"
                               Friends Journal, May 1, 1983, p. 10.

Harold Brown   "The United States Armed Forces Today," *Vital
                               Speeches of the Day*, November 15, 1980, p.
                               66.

Matthew Bunn   "Why I Refused to Register," *The Progressive*,
                               October 1980, p. 39.

Business Week   "Guns Vs. Butter," November 29, 1982, p. 68.

Eliot A. Cohen   "Why We Need a Draft," *Commentary*, April 1982,
                               p. 34.

Congressional Digest   April 1980. Entire issue debates draft
                               registration.

Conservative Digest   "How the Pentagon Wastes Your Tax Dollars,"
                               October 1982, p. 26.

                               June 1982. Section on the High Frontier and
                               conservative reactions to the peace movement.

Current History   May 1983. Entire issue devoted to the Soviet-
                               American arms race and arms control.

John C. Davis   "Economics of the Arms Race," *The Churchman*,
                               April-May 1983, p. 11.

Defense 83   A monthly magazine published by the Depart-
                               ment of Defense to provide official and pro-
                               fessional information to commanders and key
                               personnel on matters related to defense
                               policies.

Robert DeGrasse, Jr. &   "Economic Recovery Vs. Defense Spending," *USA
Paul Murphy   Today*, July 1981, p. 25.

Robert DeGrasse, Jr. &   "Megabucks for the Pentagon," *Inquiry*, April 26,
William Ragen   1982, p. 23.

219

Department of State Bulletin	May 1982. Section on arms control, including very visual atlas of current military forces.
Robert Ellsberg	"Stop This Train," *Sojourners*, June 1980, p. 20.
Engage/Social Action	February 1983. Special section on the arms race and militarization.
Gregory A. Fossedal	"The Defense Build-Up That Isn't," *Conservative Digest*, September 1982, p. 36.
Allan Dodds Frank	"The New Recruit: Motivated and Ambitious," *Forbes*, August 15, 1983, p. 30.
Milton Friedman	"High Taxes, Low Security," *Newsweek*, April 18, 1983, p. 64.
Richard A. Gabriel	"About-Face on the Draft," *America*, February 9, 1980, p. 95.
Christopher Garlock	"Why I Registered for the Draft," *The Progressive*, October 1980, p. 38.
Billy Graham	"Peace: At Times a Sword and Fire," *Christianity Today*, December 17, 1982, p. 22.
Darel Grothaus	"The Danger In Chirps and Mutters," *Sojourners*, March 1983, p. 32.
	"Scared to Death," *Sojourners*, February 1983, p. 22.
Bill Green	"Mortgaging Our Future," *Bulletin of the Atomic Scientists*, April 1983, p. 28.
Meg Greenfield	"Throwing Money at Defense," *Newsweek*, June 1, 1981, p. 98.
Morton H. Halperin	"The Rise of Militarism, the Decline of Liberty," *Christianity and Crisis*,' October 19, 1981, p. 279.
Hugh B. Hester	"Dare to Face the Cause," *The Churchman*, June-July 1983, p. 10.
William P. Hoar	"It's Time for a Tough American Foreign Policy," *American Opinion*, April 1981, p. 25.
Llewellyn D. Howell	"America's Role in the International Arena: Why Not Number Two?" *USA Today*, January 1981, p. 15.
A.S. Jefferson & Douglas Mitchell	"The State of the Army," *New Guard*, Summer 1980, p. 32.
Robert Jewett	"A Covenant with Death," *The Christian Century*, May 18, 1983, p. 477.
Michael T. Klare	"The Weinberger Revolution," *Inquiry*, September 1982, p. 25.

220

Andrew Kopkind   "The Return of Cold War Liberalism," *The Nation*, April 23, 1983, p. 495.

Roger Landrum   "Serving America: Alternatives to the Draft," *USA Today*, January 1981, p. 9.

Edward N. Luttwak   "A Critical View of the U.S. Military Establishment," *Forbes*, May 26, 1980, p. 37.

Richard McSorley   "Changing Soldiers to Objectors," *The Churchman*, November 1982, p. 17.

Robert A. Manning   "America's Newest Tripwire," *Inquiry*, January 1983, p. 22.

D. Keith Mano   "Thoughts on the Draft Resistance," *National Review*, February 18, 1983, p. 200.

Jonathan Marshall   "Who's Afraid of Defense Reform?" *Inquiry*, August 1982, p. 12.

Mary Morrell   "Blue Sky for Defense," *Engage/Social Action*, April 1982, p. 18.

Charles C. Moskos   "Making the All-Volunteer Force Work: A National Service Approach," *Foreign Affairs*, Fall 1981, p. 17.

The New Republic   "Resisters Without a Draft," December 13, 1982, p. 5.

Newsweek   "Why the Generals Can't Command," February 14, 1983, p. 22.

"Women in the Armed Forces," February 18, 1980, p. 34.

Verne Orr   "Report to the Shareholders of Defense," *Vital Speeches of the Day*, January 1, 1983, p. 162.

Michael Parenti   "More Bucks from the Bang," *The Progressive*, July 1980, p. 27.

Murray Polner   "Opening Pandora's Box," *Commonweal*, October 12, 1979, p. 553.

The Progressive   "Conscription – An Act of War," May 1980, p. 22.

Jeffrey Record   "Is Our Military Incompetent?" *Newsweek*, December 22, 1980, p. 9.

Robert B. Reich   "Hi-Tech Warfare," *The New Republic*, November 1, 1982, p. 17.

Alex Reyes   "The Draft Stalemate," *Inquiry*, July 1983, p. 10.

Leo Sandon, Jr.   "A National Service Draft," *The Christian Century*, February 18, 1981, p. 174.

221

George Schultz   "U.S. Foreign Policy: Realism and Progress," *Department of State Bulletin*, November 1982, p. 1.

Charles L. Schultze   "Economic Effects of the Defense Budget," *The Brookings Bulletin*, Fall 1981, p. 1.

Michael Specter   "Is the Volunteer Army a Failure?" *The Nation*, June 19, 1982, p. 743.

John M. Swomley, Jr.   "Conscience Versus the Draft," *Christianity & Crisis*, November 15, 1982, p. 347.

Ronald Reagan   "Peace and National Security," *Department of State Bulletin*, March 1983, p. 28.

     "Progress in the Quest for Peace and Deterrence," *Department of State Bulletin*, March 1983, p. 28.

John J. Rhodes   "The Far Side of the Hill," *Foreign Affairs*, Winter 1982/83, p. 365.

Alvin Richman   "Public Attitudes on Military Power, 1981," *Public Opinion*, December/January 1982, p. 44.

Matthew Stevenson   "The Ivied Walls of War," *The Progressive*, March 1983, p. 46.

Marvin Stone   "Is a Draft Inevitable?" *U.S. News & World Report*, July 13, 1981, p. 80.

Winston H. Taylor   "Our Militarized Society," *Engage/Social Action*, April 1982, p. 26.

Time   "On Being Citizens and Soldiers," June 9, 1980, p. 86. (A Time Essay by Lance Morrow.)

     "Reagan for the Defense," April 4, 1983, p. 8.

     "The Winds of Reform," March 7, 1983, p. 12.

Sheila Tobias & Shelah Leader   "An Intelligent Woman's Guide to the Military Mind," *Ms.*, July/August 1982, p. 118.

Stansfield Turner & George Thibault   "Preparing for the Unexpected: The Need for a New Military Strategy," *Foreign Affairs*, Fall 1982, p. 122.

U.S. News & World Report   "Should U.S. Revive the Draft?" February 11, 1980, p. 37.

Ernest Van Den Haag   "Should We Bring Home the Troops," *National Review*, June 24, 1983, p. 751.

John W. Vessey, Jr.   "The Unrelenting Growth of Soviet Military Power," *Vital Speeches of the Day*, May 15, 1983, p. 456.

Index

223

224

The Editor

David L. Bender is a history graduate from the Univerity of Minnesota. He also has an M.A. in government from St. Mary's University in San Antonio, Texas. He has taught social problems at the high school level for several years. He is the general editor of the *Opposing Viewpoints Series* and has authored many of the titles in the series.